Illicit Trade

Counterfeiting, Piracy and the Swiss Economy

OECD

BETTER POLICIES FOR BETTER LIVES

This document, as well as any data and map included herein, are without prejudice to the status of or sovereignty over any territory, to the delimitation of international frontiers and boundaries and to the name of any territory, city or area.

The statistical data for Israel are supplied by and under the responsibility of the relevant Israeli authorities. The use of such data by the OECD is without prejudice to the status of the Golan Heights, East Jerusalem and Israeli settlements in the West Bank under the terms of international law.

Note by Turkey
The information in this document with reference to "Cyprus" relates to the southern part of the Island. There is no single authority representing both Turkish and Greek Cypriot people on the Island. Turkey recognises the Turkish Republic of Northern Cyprus (TRNC). Until a lasting and equitable solution is found within the context of the United Nations, Turkey shall preserve its position concerning the "Cyprus issue".

Note by all the European Union Member States of the OECD and the European Union
The Republic of Cyprus is recognised by all members of the United Nations with the exception of Turkey. The information in this document relates to the area under the effective control of the Government of the Republic of Cyprus.

Please cite this publication as:
OECD (2021), *Counterfeiting, Piracy and the Swiss Economy*, Illicit Trade, OECD Publishing, Paris, *https://doi.org/10.1787/1f010fc9-en*.

ISBN 978-92-64-98566-7 (print)
ISBN 978-92-64-57387-1 (pdf)
ISBN 978-92-64-76390-6 (HTML)
ISBN 978-92-64-59527-9 (epub)

Illicit Trade
ISSN 2617-5827 (print)
ISSN 2617-5835 (online)

Revised version, August 2021
Details of revisions available at: *https://www.oecd.org/about/publishing/Corrigendum_Counterfeiting-Piracy-and-the-Swiss-Economy.pdf*

Photo credits: Cover Illustration © Jeffrey Fisher.

Preface

Switzerland's performance in innovation is among the best in the world, driven by strong research-intensive institutions in both the private and public sector. Hereby, intellectual property (IP) plays a key role, as the valuable goods and services produced by this knowledge-based economy benefit considerably from IP protection. As an open economy, Switzerland participates in global markets and is firmly integrated in the world economy. These factors have contributed to the nation's economic growth and high living standards. At the same time, they can expose Switzerland to the dangers of counterfeiting and piracy.

Trade in counterfeit products is a major challenge that poses a threat to Swiss rights holders, the Swiss government and society as a whole. With the objective of providing policy makers with empirical evidence to enable them to take action against this threat, this OECD report gauges the impact of the global trade in fake "Swiss made" products on the Swiss government and Swiss industry. Furthermore, it includes an in-depth analysis in four sectors: watchmaking, electrical and mechanical engineering, the fast-moving consumer goods industry, and pharmaceuticals.

The findings of the analysis are concerning. In 2018, global trade in counterfeit and pirated goods infringing Swiss IPRs decreased lawful rights holders' sales by at least CHF 4.45 billion (USD 4.48 billion), or 1.5% of Swiss exports. In addition, it reduced the tax revenue to the Swiss government by CHF 157.5 million (USD 158.4 million), equivalent to almost 0.2% of tax revenue collected. It also led to the loss of more than ten thousand jobs, representing 1.7% of all Swiss manufacturing jobs. These findings demonstrate that coordinated measures are required at international level in order to combat IP crime and counterfeit trade.

This report aims to provide important insights into the risk that counterfeiting poses to the world economy and to assist policy makers in finding optimal solutions to respond to the threat.

Catherine Chammartin,

Director General,

Swiss Federal Institute of Intellectual Property

Elsa Pilichowski,

Director,

OECD Public Governance

Foreword

Illicit trade in fake goods is a significant and growing threat in a globalised and innovation-driven economy, undermining good governance, the rule of law and citizens' trust in government. It not only has a negative impact on the sales and profits of affected firms and on the economy in general, but also poses major health and safety threats to consumers.

To provide policy makers with robust evidence about this threat, the OECD carried out a series of analytical studies that deepen our understanding of the scale and magnitude of the problem. The results have been published in a set of reports starting with Trade in Counterfeit and Pirated Goods: Mapping the Economic Impact (2016), and including the most recent ones Trends in Trade in Counterfeit and Pirated Goods (2019), and Illicit Trade in Counterfeit Pharmaceuticals (2020). As shown in these reports, trade in counterfeit and pirated goods amounted to up to 3.3% of world trade in 2016, and was an even higher share (6.8%) of imports into the EU.

This study employs an objective and quantitative methodology for such quantitative assessment of the scale and harmful effects of world trade in counterfeit goods on Swiss rights holders and the Swiss government. The analysis in this report relies primarily on a quantitative assessment using the tailored statistical methodologies developed by the OECD, drawing on data from a large dataset on customs seizures of intellectual property-infringing goods. The data refer to the pre-COVID period, and to reflect the additional dynamics introduced by the crisis, in-depth dialogues with enforcement, trade community and industry were carried out.

The findings can help both public and private sector decision-makers better understand the nature and scale of the Swiss economy's problem and develop appropriate, evidence-based policy responses.

This study was carried out under the auspices of the OECD's Task Force on Countering Illicit Trade, which focuses on evidence-based research and advanced analytics to assist policy makers in mapping and understanding the vulnerabilities exploited and created by illicit trade.

This document was approved by the Public Governance Committee via written procedure on [tbc] and prepared for publication by the OECD Secretariat.

Acknowledgements

The report was prepared by Piotr Stryszowski, Senior Economist, and Morgane Gaudiau, Economist, at the OECD Directorate for Public Governance led by Elsa Pilichowski. Florence Mouradian provided valuable knowledge and assistance to the quantitative analysis.

The authors wish to thank Hansueli Stamm, Eiman Magshoodi, Martina Freund, Nilifer Anaç and Debora Frei from the Swiss Federal Institute of Intellectual Property (IPI) for their excellent, trust-based co-operation and valuable insights.

The authors are also grateful to representatives of Swiss industry for the valuable assistance they provided. Special expressions of appreciation go to Mr. Yves Bugmann and Mr. Michel Arnoux from the Federation of the Swiss Watch Industry (FH), Ms. Doris Anthenien from the Swiss association of mechanical and electrical engineering industries (Swissmem), Mr. Reto Müller from the Swiss industry association Chemicals Pharma Life Sciences (Scienceindustries), Mr. Stanislas Barro from Novartis, as well as to Ms. Anastasia Li-Treyer from Promarca, the Swiss Association of branded goods.

Raquel Páramo and Andrea Uhrhammer provided editorial and production support.

The database on customs seizures was provided by the World Customs Organization (WCO) and supplemented with regional data submitted by the European Commission's Directorate-General for Taxation and Customs Union, the US Customs and Border Protection Agency and the US Immigration and Customs Enforcement. The authors express their gratitude for the data and for the valuable support of these institutions.

Table of contents

Tables

Figures

Boxes

Follow OECD Publications on:

http://twitter.com/OECD_Pubs

http://www.facebook.com/OECDPublications

http://www.linkedin.com/groups/OECD-Publications-4645871

http://www.youtube.com/oecdilibrary

http://www.oecd.org/oecddirect/

Executive summary

Global trade in counterfeit goods continues to grow in scope and magnitude, with multiple impacts on consumers, rights holders and governments. For consumers, counterfeiting poses dangers for health and safety. It also lowers consumer satisfaction when low-quality fake goods are unwittingly purchased. For intellectual property rights holders, counterfeiting means lost sales as well as brand erosion. For governments, counterfeiting leads to lower tax revenues and higher unemployment, as well as greater expenses in reacting to public safety threats and dealing with anti-counterfeiting legislation.

This report illustrates how trade in counterfeit and pirated goods affects the Swiss economy. It looks at the problem from two perspectives. First, it studies the magnitude and impacts of global trade in counterfeit Swiss goods[1]. Second, it explores the impact on four Swiss industries: watchmaking; the mechanical, electrical engineering and metalworking industry; the fast-moving consumer goods industry (FMCG); and the pharmaceutical industry. The analysis identifies specific product categories targeted, the main economies of origin of counterfeit goods, and the main trade routes and transit points used. The analysis also assesses the losses due to counterfeiting, in terms of forgone sales and lower profits by Swiss innovative companies, taxes forgone by the Swiss government and jobs lost in Switzerland.

The COVID-19 pandemic has affected trade in fake goods that infringe Swiss companies' IP rights. In most cases, the crisis has aggravated the existing trends, but in terms of absolute volumes, the impact seems to be rather moderate. The key trend has been the very intense abuse of the online environment, as, under confinement, consumers turn to online markets to fulfil their needs. This resulted in a massive growth in the online supply of all sorts of counterfeits, including those infringing Swiss IP. This sharp increase in fakes concerned not only medicines and personal protective equipment (PPE), but also many other goods, including watches, fast moving consumer goods, and products of the mechanical, electrical engineering and metalworking industry.

Key findings

- The total value of world trade in fake goods that infringed Swiss intellectual property (IP) amounted to as much as CHF 7 billion (USD 7.02 billion) in 2018, equivalent to 2.3% of all Swiss genuine exports.
- Among Swiss counterfeit products, watches are by far the most targeted product for counterfeiting. Other Swiss products commonly faked include clothing, leather products and footwear.
- Counterfeit and pirated goods that infringe the intellectual property rights of Swiss rights holders come mainly from China, Hong Kong (China), Singapore and Turkey.
- Over 2017-2019, about 54% of fake goods that infringe Swiss IP were sold to consumers who knew they were buying fake goods. The share of consumers who knowingly demand fake Swiss goods does not seem to recede; between 2013-2016 it amounted to 52.3%.
- Those consumers that demand genuine "Swiss made" goods, but instead receive sub-quality fakes, suffer damage calculated at CHF 2.06 billion (USD 2.07 billion) in 2018.

Impact on the Swiss economy

- In 2018, the total lost sales of Swiss IP rights holders due to trade in fake goods infringing their rights amounted to more than CHF 4.45 billion (USD 4.48 billion). The clothing, footwear, leather and related products sector experienced the highest losses (12.5% of sector's exports), followed by the watch and jewellery sector (6.1%).

- In 2018, total job losses due to trade in counterfeit goods infringing Swiss IPRs amounted to more than 10 000 people. These losses were the highest in the watch and jewellery sector, followed by clothing; footwear; leather and related products.

- Lower sales due to counterfeiting mean lower revenues for the Swiss Government from corporate income tax, personal income tax and social security contributions. Altogether, trade in counterfeit and pirated goods resulted in a reduction of Swiss public revenues estimated to equal to almost CHF 157.5 million (USD 158.4 million) in 2018.

1. Introduction

This first section provides background information on the Swiss economy as well as the main characteristics that make the Swiss economy highly vulnerable to the risk of counterfeiting. Particular attention is then paid to the different datasets used for analytical purposes. Finally, it presents the main steps of the OECD methodology underpinning the report and which allows the assessment of the value of trade in fakes and the economic impacts on sales, jobs and tax revenues.

Why is Switzerland vulnerable to counterfeiting?

Trade in counterfeit and pirated goods[2] is a growing threat that is worth approximately USD 0.5 trillion a year or around 2.5% of global imports.[3] It is becoming a longstanding problem that appears to be growing in scope and magnitude. Counterfeiting and piracy have negative impacts on the sales and profits of affected firms, as well as on the revenue, economy, health, safety and security of both governments and consumers. In addition, organised criminal groups play an increasingly important role in these activities, benefitting significantly from highly profitable counterfeiting and piracy operations.

Switzerland is an advanced economy with gross domestic product (GDP) of CHF 626 billion (USD 633 billion) in 2019. That same year, GDP per capita was about CHF 72 675 (USD 73 114), one of the highest levels for any OECD country apart from Ireland and Luxembourg (OECD, 2019[1]).

Switzerland is also an open economy. Swiss industries are highly globalised and its exports of goods and services represented 66% of GDP in 2019, way above the OECD average (29.8%). Switzerland is one of the OECD countries with the highest export intensity, reflecting the openness of its economy. Switzerland had one of the largest current account surpluses (6.7% of GDP) in the OECD in 2019, followed by the Netherlands, Denmark and Germany (OECD, 2020[2]).

The Swiss economy is well integrated into the global economy through its active participation in global value chains. Especially dynamic are those Swiss intellectual property rights (IPR)-intensive manufacturing industries that rely on service-related activities (e.g. design, research and development [R&D]). It allows these industries to upgrade their products, ensure higher quality and eventually capture more value. This includes industries such as watch manufacturing, chemicals, machinery, electrical equipment and textiles.

Switzerland is the most innovative country in the world.[4] The Swiss economy is characterised by high IPR intensity, way above the OECD average.[5] The country has outstanding research capacities and innovation potential.

Switzerland leads many R&D-related ranks. First, Switzerland had one of the highest expenditures on R&D-to-GDP ratios (OECD, 2020[3]) in the OECD in 2017,[6] at just under 3.2% – after Israel[7], Korea and Sweden. Second, it has very high shares of graduates, doctorates (3.6% in 2009, more than double the European Union [EU] average) and researchers in its overall employees. According to the European Commission (EC), it also has the highest share of scientific publications within the 10% most-cited scientific publications worldwide (15.2% in 2014 versus 11.1% for the EU average), as well as a high number of international scientific co-publications per million people.

Switzerland ranked tenth for intellectual property (IP) filing activity in 2019 (WIPO, 2019[4]). Its ranking varies according to the type of IP concerned: it came 8th for patents but 14th and 11th for trademarks and designs respectively. The World Intellectual Property Organization (WIPO) report also mentions that Switzerland is one of the countries with the highest number of patent applications per million people, just behind Japan and Korea.

The knowledge-based and innovative character of the Swiss economy, its high IP intensity and its high degree of integration within the global economy make the Swiss industry potentially vulnerable to the threat of counterfeiting and piracy. This can have damaging effects on Swiss rights owners, consumers and the Swiss government.

Indeed, the Swiss economy has been hit very hard by counterfeiting and several OECD studies document that Swiss companies are among the worst affected by this problem.[8]

This report explores the scope of the problem for Switzerland. Following a summary of the methodology used for this quantitative analysis (below), the report then provides an overview of the issue (Chapter 2), assessing the scope and volume of counterfeiting of Swiss products, the sectors and products most affected, the value of the trade in fake Swiss products and the impacts on sales, jobs and government revenue. It then turns to an industry analysis (Chapter 3), exploring the problem in-depth for four affected sectors: watchmaking, electrical and mechanical engineering, the FMCG sector and the pharmaceutical industry. Chapter 4 concludes with some general pointers for tackling the issue.

It must also be stressed that the quantitative analysis refers to the period before the COVID-19 pandemic. The pandemic has largely reshaped both – licit trade and trade in counterfeit goods – and, consequently, some initial effects on counterfeiting have already been observed. However, other lasting results on counterfeiting are expected to emerge gradually.

Given the fast pace of changes, a precise quantitative analysis of these effects has not yet been possible; however, some results have been coined in a set of discussions with enforcement officials and industry delegates and following the ongoing enforcement actions. The main changes are the accelerated transition to e-commerce and the related booming offers of counterfeits online.

The impact of the COVID-19 pandemic on the Swiss industry is discussed in more detail in Chapters 2 and 3.

Data and methodology

Quantitative analysis in this report relies principally on two sources of statistical information: i) trade statistics; and ii) seizure data; both are discussed below. These data have been complemented with additional, relevant industrial and economic data that shaped the Swiss economy's overall background. Last, the quantitative analysis was completed with qualitative research based on literature review and structure interviews with industry experts.

Trade statistics

The trade statistics are based on the United Nations (UN) Comtrade database (landed customs value). With 171 reporting economies and 247 partner economies (76 economies in addition to reporting economies), the database covers the largest part of world trade and is considered the most comprehensive trade database available. Products are registered on a six-digit Harmonised System (HS)[9] basis, meaning that the level of detail is high. Data used in this study are based on landed customs value, which is the value of merchandise assigned by customs officials. In most instances, this is the same as the transaction value appearing on accompanying invoices. Landed customs value includes the insurance and freight charges incurred when transporting goods from the economy of origin to the economy of importation.

Seizure data

Data on customs seizures originate from national customs administrations. These data are aggregated and harmonised at the national or regional level and then submitted to international agencies that hold datasets on seizures. Two agencies and two datasets will be used as inputs into the analysis of this study. These datasets were received from:

- The World Customs Organization (WCO).
- The EC Directorate-General for Taxation and Customs Union (DG TAXUD).
- The analysis in this study also uses a dataset received from the United States (US) Department of Homeland Security (DHS) containing the seizure data from US Customs and Border Protection (CBP, the US customs agency) and from US Immigration and Customs Enforcement (ICE).

Methodology

Estimating the scale and impacts of trade in fake goods that infringe Swiss IP involved a number of steps (the methodology is described in detail in Annex A):

1. **Estimating the value of counterfeit goods traded worldwide that infringe IPRs held by Swiss rights owners**. This involved selecting observations in the various customs seizure databases that refer to IPRs registered in Switzerland. As a result, our data sample is the customs seizures reported worldwide related to counterfeit products that infringe Swiss IPRs. Our sample is about 23 000 observations; for each one, we have a range of information such as the provenance economy, the destination economy, the type of counterfeit product, the value, the infringed brand, as well as the size and the transport mode. Based on this sample, a descriptive statistics analysis is carried out in Section 2.1. Note that rights holders' locations were identified using the Global Brand Database (WIPO, 2016[5]) and the PATENTSCOPE database (WIPO, 2017[6]), both provided by WIPO.

   This process allowed the value of global counterfeiting targeting the IPR of Swiss industry to be assessed by product and economy. This was done by adapting the General Trade-Related Index of Counterfeiting (GTRIC) for economies, a methodology developed in the OECD/EUIPO report (2016[7]) for exports (see Annex A). The indices included in the GTRIC matrix calculate the likelihood that a given type of counterfeit product of a brand or patent registered in Switzerland will be sold in a given destination economy.

2. **Estimating the sales losses to the Swiss manufacturing industry**. This step determines what share of these counterfeit products is traded on either primary or secondary markets worldwide. We assume that there are at least two submarkets for counterfeit goods, referred to as the primary and secondary markets. In the primary market, consumers do not know that they are buying fakes whereas, in the secondary market, consumers knowingly buy fakes. Based on the estimates of flows of imports of counterfeits infringing Swiss IPR, the values of those products sold in the primary and secondary markets are estimated for each industry. This is done on the assumption that every sale of a fake item on a primary market represents a direct loss for the retail and wholesale industry. For secondary markets, where only a share of consumers would have deliberately substituted their purchases of counterfeit products for legitimate ones, the analysis is based on proxies of consumers' substitution rates, i.e. the extent to which every knowing purchase of a non-genuine product displaces a legal sale (OECD, 2017[8]). The estimates for substitution rates in the secondary market used in this analysis are presented in Table A.1. For more information about the primary and secondary markets, see Annex A.1.

Table 1.1. Assumed consumer substitution rates in the main scenario

Sector	Substitution rate (%)
Perfumery and cosmetics	49
Watches and jewellery	27
Clothing, accessories, leather and related products	39
Other sectors	32

Note: With respect to watches and jewellery, a substitution rate of 27% has been determined. This means that every USD 1 spent on fake watches and jewellery in the secondary market translates into USD 0.27 in lost sales for the manufacturing industry.
Source: Anti-Counterfeiting Group (2007[9]), *Consumer Survey*, www.wipo.int/ip-outreach/en/tools/research/details.jsp?id=691; Tom, G. et al. (1998[10]), "Consumer demand for counterfeit goods", *Psychology & Marketing*, Vol. 15/5, pp. 405-421.

Within secondary markets, these substitution rates are applied. For each industry, this yields the lost sales of Swiss rights' holders. In other words, the estimated value of products sold worldwide that are fake versions of these Swiss brands is combined with information on: i) the share of primary and secondary markets for these products by destination economy; and ii) consumers' substitution rates. The total value of lost sales for Swiss rights' holders is calculated by adding the value of sales of fake products on primary markets to the value of sales on the secondary market, adjusted for consumers' substitution rates.

3. **Estimating job and tax losses**. This step estimates the job losses in the Swiss manufacturing sector in response to lost sales on export markets and domestically as a result of counterfeiting. This is done by applying the econometric model presented in detail in the OECD report on the United Kingdom (UK) economy (OECD, 2017[8]).

The estimates of the sales elasticity of employment for each Swiss manufacturing industry are reported in Table 1.2. Again, a decrease in sales does not translate into the same proportion of lost jobs in each sector. For instance, a 1% decline in sales in the food, beverage and tobacco industry induces a 0.79% decline in the number of employees within this sector, whereas a 1% decline in sales in the clothing, footwear and leather industry would see a 0.52% decrease in employees. These sales-jobs transmission rates can be used to estimate the share of lost jobs due to the counterfeiting of Swiss products. For each Swiss manufacturing sector, this is done by multiplying the transmission rate by the share of lost sales for Swiss IPR owners.

Table 1.2. Elasticity of employment linked to sales in the Swiss manufacturing sector

Sector	Sales elasticity of employment
Food, beverages and tobacco	0.787
Chemical and allied products; except pharmaceuticals, perfumery and cosmetics	0.631
Pharmaceutical and medicinal chemical products	0.691
Textiles and other intermediate products (e.g. plastics; rubbers; paper; wood)	0.824
Clothing, footwear, leather and related products	0.523
Watches and jewellery	0.673
Non-metallic mineral products (e.g. glass and glass products, ceramic products)	0.647
Basic metals and fabricated metal products (except machinery and equipment)	0.820
Electrical household appliances, electronic and telecommunications equipment	0.768
Machinery, industrial equipment; computers and peripheral equipment; ships and aircraft	0.813
Motor vehicles and motorcycles	0.472
Household cultural and recreation goods, including toys and games, books and musical instruments	0.181
Furniture, lighting equipment, carpets and other manufacturing n.e.c*	0.697

Note: All the figures refer to the elasticity of employment for each industry following a 1% decline in sales. For instance, a 1% decline in sales in the food, beverage and tobacco industry induces a 0.79% decline in the number of employees within this sector.
* Not elsewhere classified.

These transmission rates between sales and jobs can be used to estimate the share of lost jobs due to infringements in the global trade of Swiss IP in total employment. For each Swiss manufacturing industry, this is done by multiplying the transmission rate with the share of lost sales for Swiss IPR owners.

It is worth noting that our study only focuses on job losses in Switzerland but ignores the job losses in other countries where Swiss rights holders may hold a factory.

Theoretically, four types of tax revenue losses occur in Switzerland due to infringement of Swiss IP: value-added taxes (VAT); corporate income taxes (CIT) of rights holders; personal income taxes (PIT); and social security contributions (SSC) paid by employers and employees. Lower sales of genuine products due to counterfeit and pirated imports reduce mainly the latter three sources of revenue for the Swiss government:

- CIT that would have been collected from firms in the wholesale and retail industry.
- SSC that would have been paid by employees and employers in the retail and wholesale industry.
- PIT of employees and employers that would have been collected in the manufacturing industry.

These three sources of lost revenues are calculated for each manufacturing sector in order to estimate the results as accurately as possible. The overall national result was obtained by adding the estimated amounts of tax revenues foregone for each sector.

Government taxes lost from CIT are calculated by multiplying the average profit rates for each category of the manufacturing industry by the average rate of corporation tax, taking into account the estimated value of lost sales.

SSC losses are calculated by multiplying the share of the actual average amount of SSC paid by employees and employers per unit of employment by the number of estimated jobs lost due to counterfeit and pirated imports.

The PIT foregone is calculated by multiplying the average salary in each industry by the average income tax rate times the number of lost jobs.

Although VAT losses are not fully experienced by the Swiss government since most fake Swiss goods are purchased abroad, an estimation of VAT losses is provided. This illustrates the amount of VAT losses that might be reached if Swiss counterfeit products were purchased domestically. Lost VAT is calculated by applying the VAT rates to the estimated amount of total lost sales due to counterfeit and pirated imports.

References

Anti-Counterfeiting Group (2007), *Consumer Survey*, http://www.wipo.int/ip-outreach/en/tools/research/details.jsp?id=691. [9]

OECD (2020), "Gross domestic spending on R&D (indicator)", https://doi.org/10.1787/d8b068b4-en (accessed on 26 April 2019). [3]

OECD (2020), "Trade in goods and services (indicator)", https://doi.org/10.1787/0fe445d9-en (accessed on 26 April 2019). [2]

OECD (2019), "Gross domestic product (GDP) (indicator)", https://doi.org/10.1787/dc2f7aec-en (accessed on 26 April 2019). [1]

OECD (2017), *Trade in Counterfeit Products and the UK Economy: Fake Goods, Real Losses*, OECD Publishing, Paris, http://dx.doi.org/10.1787/9789264279063-en. [8]

OECD/EUIPO (2019), *Trends in Trade in Counterfeit and Pirated Goods*, Illicit Trade, OECD Publishing, Paris, https://doi.org/10.1787/g2g9f533-en. [11]

OECD/EUIPO (2016), *Trade in Counterfeit and Pirated Goods: Mapping the Economic Impact*, OECD Publishing, Paris, http://dx.doi.org/10.1787/9789264252653-en. [7]

Tom, G. et al. (1998), "Consumer demand for counterfeit goods", *Psychology and Marketing*, Vol. 15/5, pp. 405-421. [10]

WIPO (2019), *Intellectual Property Indicators 2019*, World Intellectual Property Organization, Geneva, https://www.wipo.int/publications/en/details.jsp?id=4369. [4]

WIPO (2017), *PATENTSCOPE Database: International and National Patent Collection*, World Intellectual Property Organization, Geneva. [6]

WIPO (2016), *Global Brand Database*, World Intellectual Property Organization, Geneva, https://www3.wipo.int/branddb/en/. [5]

Notes

[1] In this study, we understand a "Swiss" or "Swiss Made" product to be a product that bears the trademark or other intellectual property right of a Swiss company.

[2] Counterfeit and pirated products are defined as goods that infringe trademarks, copyrights, patents or design rights.

[3] See OECD/EUIPO (2016[7]).

[4] See http://www.wipo.int/econ_stat/en/economics/gii/.

[5] See OECD (2015), *OECD Science, Technology and Industry Outlook 2014*, "OECD Science, Technology and Industry Outlook 2014", *OECD Science, Technology and R&D Statistics (database)*, https://doi.org/10.1787/139a90c6-en and OECD (2013), *Supporting Investment in Knowledge Capital, Growth and Innovation*, OECD Publishing, Paris, https://doi.org/10.1787/9789264193307-en.

[6] Latest data available for Switzerland.

[7] The statistical data for Israel are supplied by and under the responsibility of the relevant Israeli authorities. The use of such data by the OECD is without prejudice to the status of the Golan Heights, East Jerusalem and Israeli settlements in the West Bank under the terms of international law.

[8] See OECD/EUIPO (2019[11]) and OECD/EUIPO (2016[7]).

[9] The Harmonised System (HS) is an international commodity classification system, developed and maintained by the World Customs Organization (WCO).

2. An overview of global counterfeiting and the Swiss economy

This chapter appraises the damage caused by infringement of Swiss intellectual property rights in world trade. It identifies who suffers in particular from this illicit activity, estimates the scope and volume of such infringements, and presents the top destination and provenance economies for counterfeit goods that infringe Swiss IPR. The focus then shifts to the Swiss products that are most susceptible to counterfeiting. This chapter also pays particular attention to the latest trends in trade in counterfeit goods infringing Swiss IPR related to the COVID-19 pandemic. Finally, the negative effects of IPR infringement on the Swiss economy are estimated in terms of lost sales, lost jobs, and lost government revenue.

The scope and magnitude of the problem

Where do fake Swiss products originate?

Over the 2011-19 period, the largest share of fake Swiss products seized infringing Swiss intellectual property (IP) originated from the People's Republic of China (hereinafter China) and Hong Kong (China). In 2016, these economies represented 52% and 25% of customs seizures respectively. In terms of seized value, China and Hong Kong (China) also accounted for the largest share of counterfeit Swiss products. In 2016, China accounted for more than 70% of seized value while Hong Kong (China) represented 19%.

Over the 2017-19 period, China and Hong Kong (China) remained the main provenance countries of fake Swiss products in terms of both customs seizures and seized value, followed by Turkey and Singapore.

An important observation is the strengthening of the role of Hong Kong (China) as an important transit hub for fake Swiss products. In 2019, this economy accounted for almost 70% of the total seized value of fake Swiss products while China accounted for 18% (Figure 2.1).

Figure 2.1. Top provenance economies of fake goods infringing Swiss IP, 2017-19

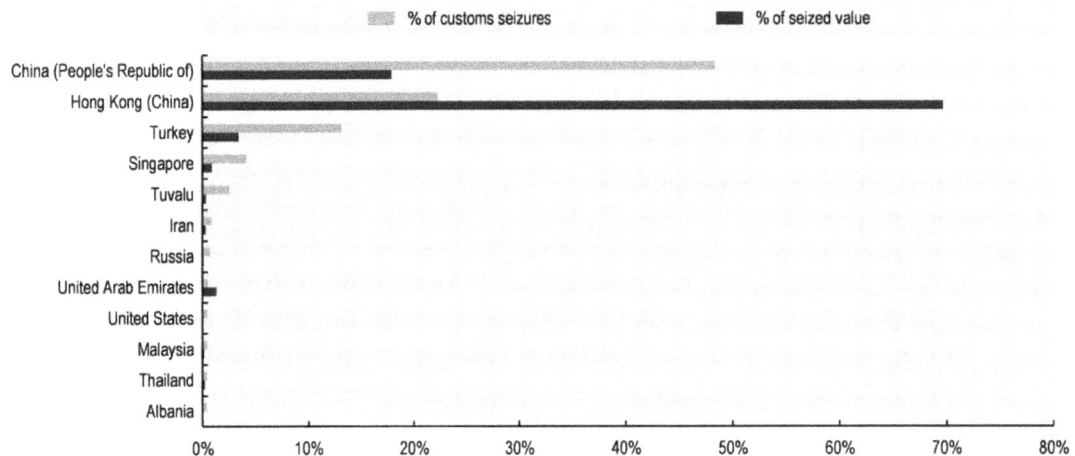

Note: Tuvalu is a seasonal transit point, misused by traffickers in their operations.
Source: OECD customs seizures database.

Figure 2.2 lists the other top source economies of fake goods infringing Swiss IP excluding China and Hong Kong (China) (the main provenance countries). This reveals the relative roles of subsidiary economies as sources of fake Swiss products.

Figure 2.2. Other main provenance economies of fake Swiss goods, excluding China and Hong Kong (China), 2017-19

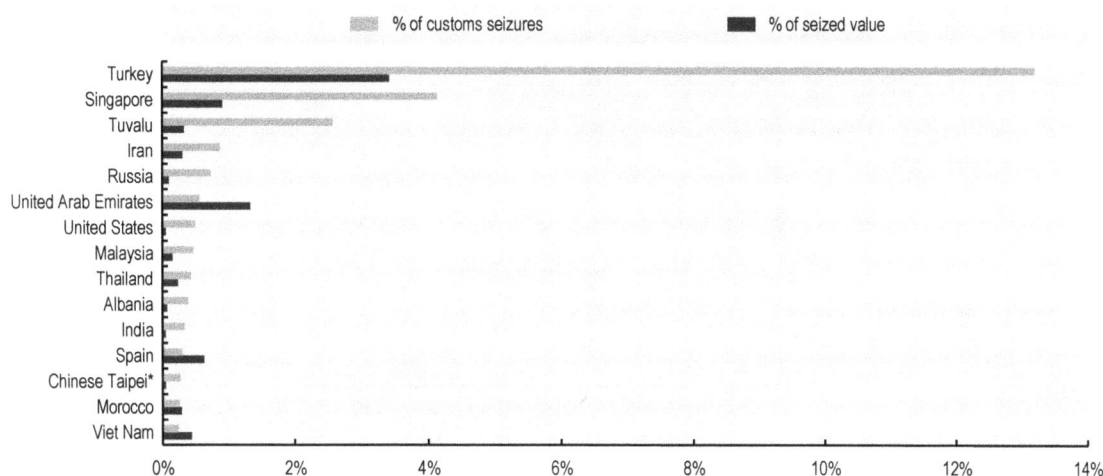

Source: OECD customs seizures database.

The list of secondary sources of fake goods that infringe Swiss IP changes very dynamically. It also includes some small countries that appear as seasonal transit economies for fake products (e.g. Tuvalu). It reinforces the points made in the OECD/EUIPO studies,[1] that the trade routes of fake goods are very dynamic, as counterfeiters adapt their strategies instantly, quickly responding to enforcement actions taken by customs. It also points out the great difficulty and complexity involved in countering this scourge.

Which product categories are targeted most?

There are two relevant measures that show the intensity of trade in fakes in different product categories: number of seizures and value of products seized. Counterfeit products infringing Swiss IP were mostly watches, representing around 80% of both seized value and customs seizures.

In terms of number of seizures, other than watches, clothing (11.4% of customs seizures), and footwear (3.2%) were the main counterfeit product categories seized (Figure 2.3).

In terms of value, clothing (3.8%) and articles of leather (2%) were the main categories seized after watches.

The difference between the seized value and the number of customs seizures can be explained by the varying unit value of goods (for instance a single luxury product that deceives customers can be of relatively high value). It can also be attributed to transport modes and the related size of shipment. For tobacco, for example, the difference comes from some seizures of vessels containing large quantities of cigarettes: around one-third of seizures of tobacco infringing Swiss IPRs contained more than 16 000 items. Such quantities tend to increase the seized value, while they still count as a single seizure. Conversely, for clothing, only a few seizures related to shipment by sea have been made and the size of a single shipment tends to be small.

Another worrying trend is counterfeit packaging and logos. The number of seizures of these items keeps growing – in 2019, they accounted for about 3% of total seizures. Counterfeit packaging illustrates a growing trend when counterfeiters smuggle an unbranded good and a logo separately, to reduce the risk of a seizure. Even though the good might still violate some IP rights, like patents or designs, the risk of detection is much smaller than in the case of a counterfeit product. As noted by enforcement officials and industry experts, this tactic has recently become frequently used by counterfeiters targeting Swiss branded products.

Figure 2.3. Top Swiss products targeted by counterfeiting, 2017-19

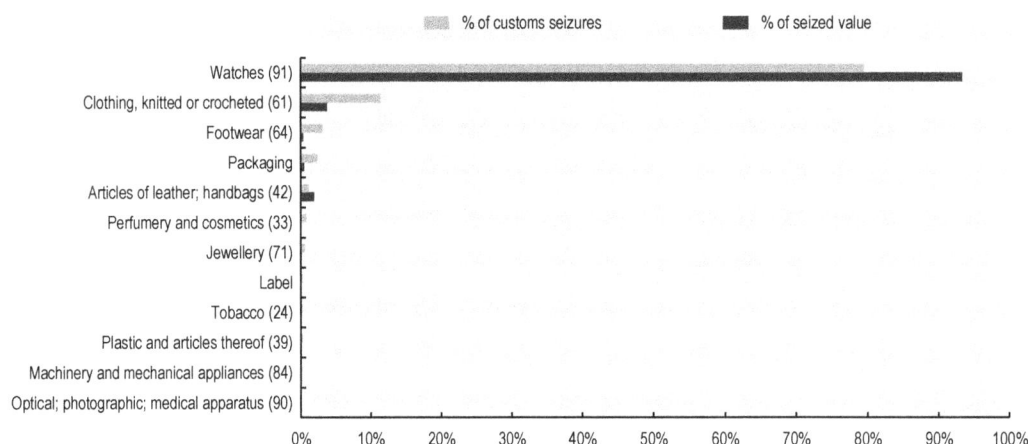

Note: Figures in parenthesis are Harmonised System (HS) codes as defined by United Nations (UN) Trade Statistics (2017).
Source: OECD customs seizures database.

Figure 2.4. Other Swiss product categories targeted by counterfeiting, excluding watches, 2017-19

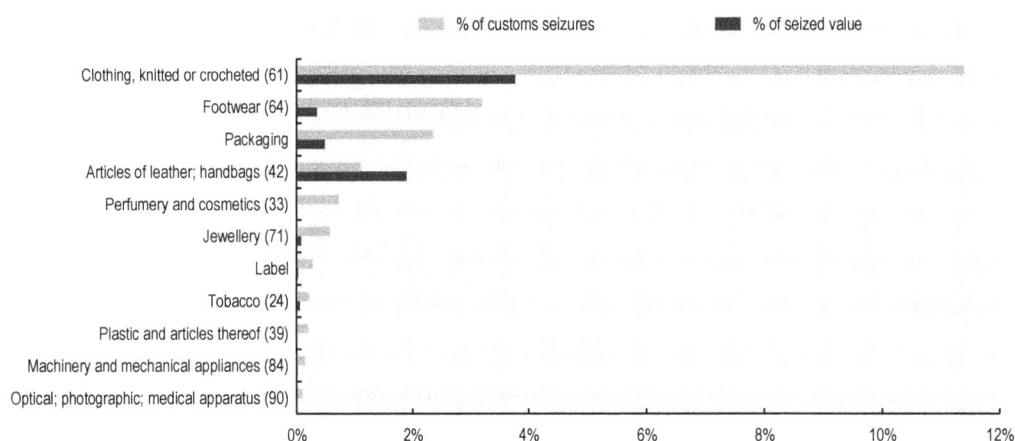

Note: Figures in parenthesis are Harmonised System (HS) codes as defined by United Nations (UN) Trade Statistics (2017).
Source: OECD customs seizures database.

What are the main destinations for Swiss fakes?

Fakes infringing Swiss IP were exported to 55 different economies between 2017 and 2019 – though mainly European countries (Figure 2.5). Germany (48%) and Belgium (14%) were the main destination economies for these fakes, followed by the Netherlands, the United Kingdom (UK) and Spain.

In terms of seized value, the ranking is different, with the UK being the main destination country, representing more than 60% of the seized value. The UK was followed by Germany (11.4%) and the Netherlands (5.5%).

The big differences between the share of seized value and the share of customs seizures can be explained by the transport mode used to export the fake Swiss goods. Indeed, sea transport was more often used to export fake Swiss goods to Belgium and the UK, while Swiss fake goods destined for Germany were mainly shipped by mail. This means that the size of shipments of fake Swiss goods exported to the UK tend to be big while the size of shipments exported to Germany was smaller.

Figure 2.5. Top destinations of counterfeit goods infringing Swiss IP, 2017-19

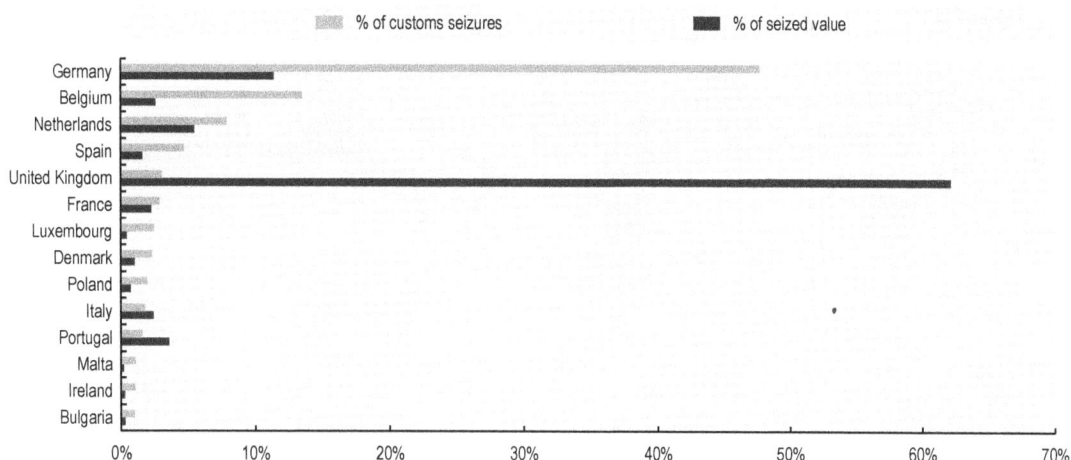

Source: OECD customs seizures database

The preponderance of European countries as destinations for fake Swiss goods is partly explained by the nature of the dataset on customs seizures. As indicated in Chapter 1 the data on customs seizures rely on three sources: the World Customs Office, EC Directorate-General for Taxation and Customs Union (DG TAXUD), the United States (US) Customs and Border Protection and the US Immigration and Customs Enforcement (CBP/ICE). The latter source does not provide the name of infringed brands. Consequently, data relative to counterfeit goods seized in the US are outside the scope of the analysis of Swiss IP infringement.

In order to address this bias, we need to estimate how many fake Swiss products are destined for the US. This estimation is done for each product category. To do this we assume that the share of fake Swiss products worldwide is the same as in the US. Take the example of fake watches: of all fake watches, around 55% are fakes of Swiss products. We can therefore assume that 55% of fake watches seized by US customs are fake Swiss products.

Based on these assumptions, the US would be the top destination country of counterfeit Swiss goods: however, this result is based on strong assumptions and has to be interpreted with caution.

How are fake Swiss goods exported?

Over the whole analysed period, for which robust data are available, i.e. between 2011 and 2018, small parcels sent by mail were the predominant way of exporting fake "Swiss made" goods.

As presented in Figure 2.6, between 2011 and 2016, most fake Swiss goods were sent by mail (49% of customs seizures), followed by air transport and express courier, at 30% and 14% of seizures respectively.[2] In terms of value, air and sea transport were the main modes of transport for counterfeit goods infringing Swiss IPRs.

This trend of abuse of small parcels continued over the 2017-19 period when mail (67%) and air transport (18%) were also the preferred conveyance methods of fake Swiss goods. In terms of value, sea and express courier were the main modes of transport for counterfeit goods infringing Swiss IPRs as air transport has declined compared to the 2011-16 period.

Figure 2.6. Modes of transporting counterfeit Swiss products

2011-2016

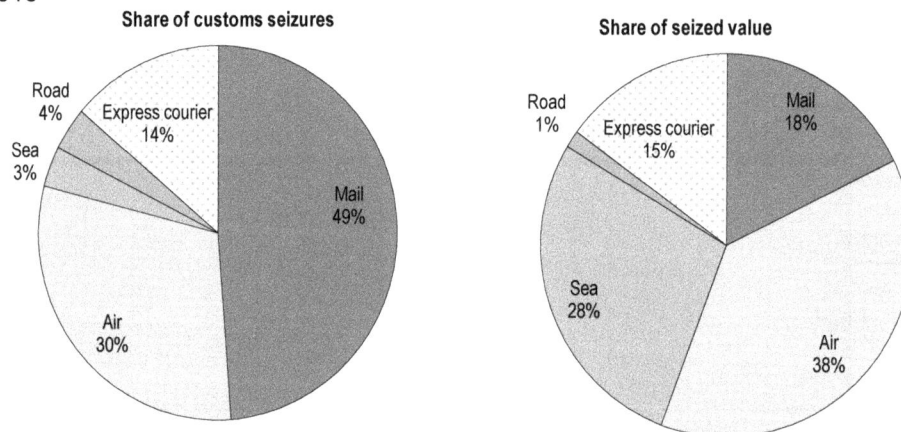

2017-2019

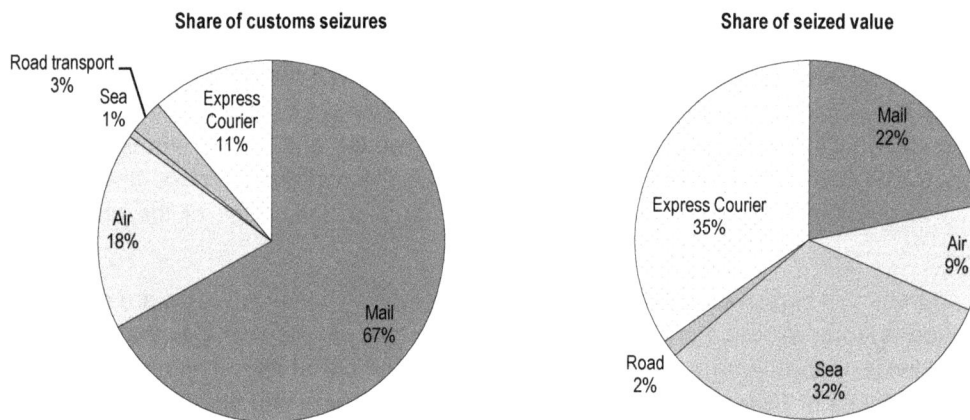

Source: OECD customs seizures database

During the analysed period, most shipments of counterfeit Swiss products appear to be small). Almost 70% of customs seizures registered report only 1 item per shipment; 84% of shipments contained fewer than 6 items.

Over the 2017-19 period, the shipment size of counterfeit Swiss goods was stable compared to 2011-16. Small shipments dominated the trade in counterfeit Swiss goods: they represented 70% of customs seizures of Swiss counterfeit products.

Figure 2.7. Counterfeit goods infringing Swiss IP, by size of shipment, 2011-16 and 2017-19 (as a share of customs seizures)

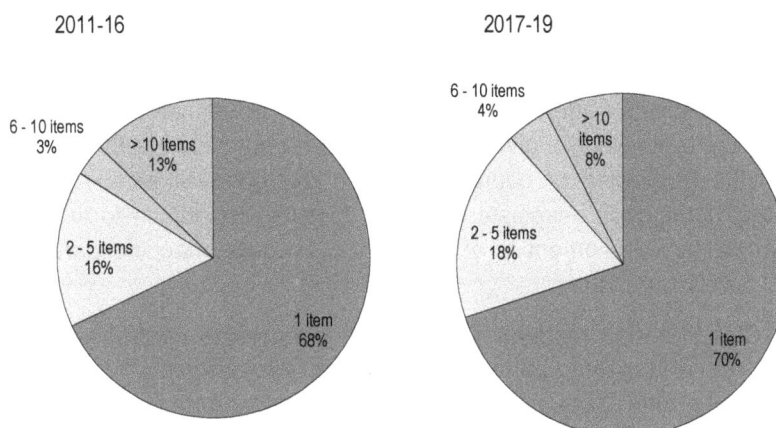

2011-16

2017-19

6 - 10 items
3%

> 10 items
13%

2 - 5 items
16%

1 item
68%

6 - 10 items
4%

> 10 items
8%

2 - 5 items
18%

1 item
70%

Source: OECD customs seizures database

COVID-19 and fake "Swiss made"

The COVID-19 pandemic has largely reshaped the dynamics of routes of illicit trade, including illicit trade in counterfeit "Swiss made" goods. Consequently, some short-term impacts have been already identified in a set of discussions with enforcement officials and industry delegates. Other lasting results on counterfeiting are expected to emerge gradually.

As for the short-term effects, trade and enforcement experts highlight that the pandemics has intensified existing problems and, in terms of volumes, there are some modest effects. Experts also point at several COVID-19-related factors that have shaped the landscape of illicit trade for fake "Swiss made" products, such as changing trade routes and distorted supply chains.

Criminal networks have reacted very quickly to the crisis and adapted their strategies to take advantage of the shifting landscape. In many cases, criminals have foreseen the disruptions of some transport routes and managed their operations accordingly, for example intensifying supply through small parcels on those routes where traffic remained open. For example, in the initial stage of the pandemics, Asian countries were locked down and, consequently, traditional trade routes from Asia to Europe and the US have experienced disruptions. At that same time, enforcement reported unusual activity of traffickers abusing new routes, for example through some African and Latin American countries. This was also the case of fake "Swiss made" products that kept flooding Europe and the US through remaining trade channels.

The dynamic behaviour of criminals running illicit trade networks results in a substantial shift towards further misuse of the online environment. According to law enforcement authorities, in OECD countries including Switzerland, e-commerce has become a predominant medium to send counterfeit products to consumers, as during confinements, people turn to online markets to fulfil their needs. The online boom also resulted in a considerable growth of new online marketplaces and online platforms offering fake goods. In addition to online shops, criminals abuse other online channels of communication, for example, social media platforms or communicators, such as WhatsApp or Facebook Messenger.

In all these channels, there is robust observable growth in the online supply of fake "Swiss made" goods. This includes watches, products of the mechanical, electrical engineering and metalworking (MEM) industry, fast-moving consumer goods (FMCG) and pharmaceuticals. It occurs on all types of online platforms, including those that used to be relatively free from this risk before the COVID-19 crisis. For example, in 2020, the Federation of the Swiss Watch Industry's (FH) Internet Enforcement Team closed more than 1.2 million offers for fake watches on numerous Internet sales platforms.

Finally, due to the pandemic, the demand for pharmaceuticals and personal protective equipment (PPE, for example masks, safety glasses, protective clothing) grew sharply. Very strong demand for these products was met with a strong and diverse reaction for counterfeiters. To improve the appearance of the fake PPE, criminals abuse existing trademarks of trusted Swiss companies and put their brands on fake PPE. This is often the case even when a given Swiss firm does not produce PPE of this particular kind. This clearly illustrates the free-riding of counterfeiters on the goodwill established by Swiss FMCG companies and trust that consumers associate with their brands. In addition to the PPE, criminals also supply counterfeit, substandard equipment to produce PPE or spare machine parts, which in all cases infringe the IP rights of Swiss companies.

At the same time, COVID-19 also resulted in changes in customs control priorities (e.g. focus on COVID-19-related products) and labour shortages among law enforcement officials. Unfortunately, these factors reduce enforcement efforts to counter illicit trade in many counterfeit products,

The industry continues to combat this scourge actively through many channels. For example, some industry associations offer online training for enforcement authorities to assist them with COVID-19 challenges.

Box 2.1. Stop Piracy

Stop Piracy is a public-private initiative established to raise awareness and counter IP infringements. It brings together Swiss public authorities and representatives of the Swiss industry.

The initiative raises awareness by providing targeted educational consumer campaigns, e.g. before Christmas or Black Friday, highlighting the risk of counterfeits in a factual and objective way. It also provides a platform for dialogue and co-ordination between delegates from the Swiss federal administration (e.g. the Intellectual Property Institute or Swiss Federal Customs Administration) and Swiss industry delegates.

Source: https://www.stop-piracy.ch/.

Another example of a public-private partnership to counter the threat of counterfeiting aimed at Swiss products is the Stop Piracy initiative (see Box 2.1.). This initiative was established before the pandemic for co-ordination and as awareness-raising. During the COVID-19 crisis, Stop Piracy continued its activities, raising awareness about the scourge of counterfeiting.

The value of trade in fake Swiss goods

So far, the analysis has relied on descriptive statistics of customs seizures of counterfeit products that infringe Swiss IPRs. The following section is based on econometric analysis and aims at assessing the value of fake Swiss goods as well as determining the shares of primary and secondary markets for counterfeit goods infringing Swiss IPRs.

As explained in Annex A, applying the General Trade-Related Index of Counterfeiting for economies (GTRIC-e) and for products (GTRIC-p),[3] as well as a fixed point to data on Swiss exports, allows the absolute values to be gauged for trade in counterfeit and pirated goods infringing the IPR owned by Swiss residents. The GTRIC-e and GTRIC-p indices offer an estimate of the probability of each product and trading partner being counterfeited. In the framework of this study, the watches destined for European countries are likely to have the highest probability of being counterfeited relative to other product category-destination couples. To estimate the value of fake trade infringing Swiss IPRs, the share of counterfeit goods in total exports in a selected product category from a given trade partner has to be known. We call this percentage the "fixed point". Based on customs expertise, the fixed point has been established at 27% for Harmonised System (HS) code 64 (footwear) from China, which is the product-provenance couple most likely to be counterfeited. This fixed point has to be considered as the upper limit of counterfeit trade. We also carried out additional checks to verify if this fixed point was robust. To do so, the empirical application was based on 3 scenarios, with selected values of 10%, 15% and 20%. Note that all of these scenarios take much more conservative values of fixed points than the actual fixed points applied to imports in OECD/EUIPO reports (2016[7]; 2019[11]). For other product-provenance couples, a more conservative fixed point is used; for product-provenance couples other than footwear from China, these fixed points are applied. In the text, these fixed points are named "ceiling values".

Thus, the fixed point is basically multiplied by the relative likelihood included in the GTRIC matrix to obtain the share of exports of counterfeit products infringing Swiss IPRs. Applying these shares to statistics on the value of Swiss exports gives the estimated value of goods infringing Swiss IPRs by product category and destination economy.

Table 2.1 reports the estimated value of global trade in counterfeit products infringing Swiss trademarks and patents for 2016-19 for these three alternative ceiling values. The best estimates, based on the data provided by customs authorities worldwide and on the GTRIC methodology, indicate that global trade in counterfeit and pirated products infringing Swiss trademarks and patents amounted to as much as CHF 6.97 billion (USD 7 billion) in 2018, equivalent to 2.3% of Swiss genuine exports of goods. The value of fakes varies from year to year and it reflects customs profiling procedure that may vary over time.

Table 2.1. Estimated value of global trade in counterfeit Swiss products, 2016-19

	2016		2017		2018		2019	
	Value in USD billion	Share of genuine exports (%)	Value in USD billion	Share of genuine exports (%)	Value in USD billion	Share of genuine exports (%)	Value in USD billion	Share of genuine exports (%)
Ceiling value 20%	5.40	1.8%	2.33	0.8%	7.02	2.3%	5.24	1.7%
Ceiling value 15%	4.06	1.3%	1.75	0.6%	5.26	1.7%	3.93	1.3%
Ceiling value 10%	2.71	0.9%	1.17	0.4%	3.51	1.1%	2.62	0.8%

Note: The value for 2019 is still being refined.

In a previous report that focused on the Italian market (OECD, 2018[12]), the OECD indicated that the value of global trade in counterfeit Italian products amounted to USD 35 billion in 2016, equivalent to 7.6% of total Italian goods exports. The same OECD report dedicated to trade in counterfeit goods and the Swedish economy (OECD, 2019[13]) estimated the value of global trade in counterfeit Swedish products at USD 3.4 billion or 2.4% of Swedish goods exports.

It should be pointed out that the comparisons of the absolute values in fake trade have to be interpreted carefully. Indeed, the infringed products differ from country to country. For Switzerland, the most infringed product is mainly luxury watches while clothing and bearing is the most targeted product for Italy and Sweden respectively. Such a difference has necessary consequences on the total values of global counterfeiting trade infringing residents' IPRs.

Figure 2.8 shows the estimated absolute value in global trade for the main counterfeit product categories. The Swiss watchmaking industry remained by far the most targeted by counterfeiters over the 2017-19 period. The estimated value of fake Swiss watches accounted for CHF 3.35 billion (USD 3.37 billion) in 2018, which represented almost 50% of the total value of fake trade in counterfeit Swiss goods.

In relative terms, clothing, footwear, leather and related products were again the most often counterfeited type of products in 2018. The fake products in this category represented almost 17% of all export categories. As in previous years, they were followed by watches and jewellery (10.2%) and food, beverages and tobacco (5%).

Figure 2.8. Most faked Swiss product categories in global trade, 2018

In terms of value

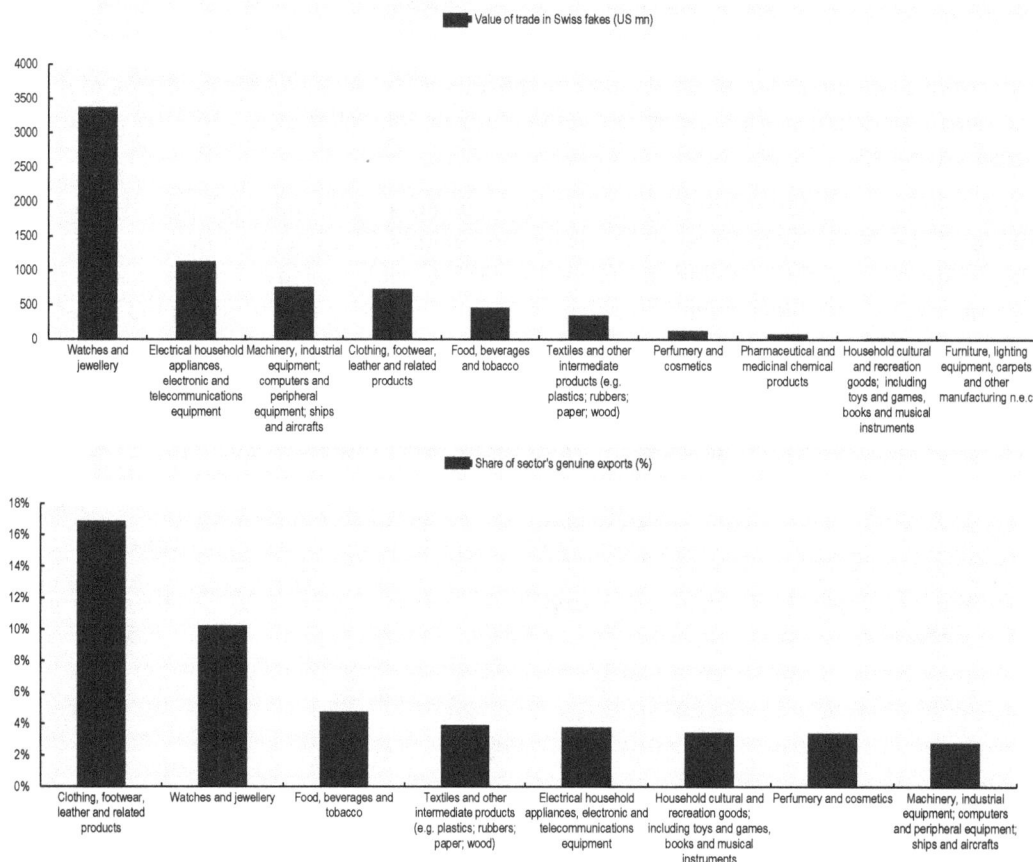

The secondary market

We assume that there are at least two submarkets for counterfeit goods, the primary and secondary markets. In the primary market, consumers do not know that they are buying fakes, whereas, in the secondary market, consumers knowingly buy fakes. The two markets are characterised by price differences. The primary market's prices are expected to be close to genuine goods while the secondary market's prices are expected to be lower. To determine the share of both markets, we analysed the unit values of fake goods that we consider to be proxies for retail prices (for more detailed information, see Annex A.1)

In terms of consumer deception, the analysis shows that, in 2016, 47.7% of Swiss fakes traded worldwide were sold on the primary market, i.e. they were sold to consumers who did not know they were buying fake products. Conversely, 52.3% of the Swiss counterfeit goods traded worldwide were sold on the secondary market, i.e. they were sold to consumers who knowingly buy fakes.

Over the 2017-19 period, the share of secondary markets is quite similar as in 2011-16 (see Table 2.2.). Indeed, 54.1% of counterfeit goods infringing Swiss IP were sold on the secondary market versus 52.3% over the 2011-16 period. The share of the secondary market varies considerably from one sector to another, ranging from almost 65% for the machinery, industrial equipment, computer and peripheral equipment, ships and aircraft sector to 16.7% for the furniture, lighting equipment, carpets and other manufacturing sectors. These results are quite logical since the share of the secondary market (i.e. the share of consumers who knowingly bought fakes) is lower for products that might directly damage health such as foodstuffs or cosmetics.

Table 2.2. Share of secondary markets for counterfeit Swiss products, 2017-19

Sector	Share of secondary market (%)
Electrical household appliances, electronic and telecommunications equipment	49.5
Clothing, footwear, leather and related products	42.7
Household cultural and recreation goods; including toys and games, books and musical instruments	37.5
Textiles and other intermediate products (e.g. plastics; rubbers; paper; wood)	34.2
Food, beverages and tobacco	32.7
Perfumery and cosmetics	26.5
Furniture, lighting equipment, carpets and other manufacturing n.e.c*	16.7
Total	**54.1**

Note: 54.1% of counterfeit goods infringing Swiss IP were sold to consumers who knew they were buying fake products.
* Not elsewhere classified.
Source: OECD customs seizures database

Once the primary and secondary markets have been determined, the rate of consumer deception can be estimated. Consumers in the primary market, who unwittingly purchase fake Swiss goods, pay an excessive price for a low-quality product, while consumers in the secondary market who knowingly purchase fake products are prepared to accept any trade-off between cost and quality. As explained in Annex A.6, the consumer detriment can be estimated by the difference between the average price on the primary market and the average price on the secondary market, multiplied by the volume of fake goods sold on the primary market.

The estimates of consumer detriment caused by Swiss IP infringement are presented in Table 2.3. One should note that the consumer detriment will not only focus on Swiss consumers – as Switzerland is not the main destination for counterfeit goods that infringe Swiss IP – but on all consumers located worldwide that have bought fake Swiss goods. Apart from overpayment, consuming fake goods might be dangerous for safety or health. However, this is outside the scope of this study, as are other impacts such as long-run effects due to brand erosion or unemployment burden.

In 2018, the total consumer detriment due to trade in counterfeit goods infringing Swiss IPRs amounted to CHF 1.98 billion (USD 2 billion). The consumer detriment of fake Swiss watches accounted for almost CHF 1.79 billion (USD 1.8 billion) and was followed by the electrical household appliances and electronic and telecommunication equipment CHF 140.2 million (USD 141 million) and clothing, footwear, leather and related products CHF 127.2 million (USD 128 million).

Table 2.3. Estimate of consumer detriment from counterfeit Swiss goods, 2018'

Sector	USD mn
Clothing, footwear, leather and related products	128
Watches and jewellery	1790
Electrical household appliances, electronic and telecommunications equipment	141
Household cultural and recreation goods; including toys and games, books and musical instruments	9.4

Impacts on sales, jobs and government revenue

Following the methodology (steps 2 and 3) introduced in Chapter 1, the subsequent sections are dedicated to assessing the impacts of Swiss IPR infringements on the Swiss economy.

Impact on sales in the Swiss manufacturing industry

In 2018, the total lost sales due to trade in counterfeit goods infringing Swiss IPRs amounted to CHF 4.45 billion (USD 4.48 billion). The watch and jewellery sector experienced the highest losses in absolute terms in 2018 and 2016 as well. In 2018, the sales losses of this industry amounted to CHF 1.99 billion (USD 2 billion) while they were slightly lower in 2016 at CHF 1.65 billion (USD 1.66 billion).

In relative terms, the clothing, footwear, leather and related products sector experienced the highest losses (12.5% of sector's exports) followed by the watches and jewellery (6.1%) and food, beverages and tobacco (3.7%) sectors. In 2016, these three sectors were also the most impacted in relative terms. However, this year the food, beverages and tobacco sector experienced the highest losses in relative terms (9% of exports), followed by the clothing, footwear, leather and related products sector (8.1%) and the watch and jewellery sector (5.5%) (see Table 2.4)

Table 2.4. Estimated lost sales for most targeted Swiss manufacturing industries, 2016 and 2018

	2016		2018	
	Sales losses in USD million	Share of exports (%)	Sales losses in USD million	Share of exports (%)
Food, beverages and tobacco	799.5	9.0	355.4	3.7
Perfumery and cosmetics	56.9	1.9	109.0	2.9
Textiles and other intermediate products (e.g. plastics; rubbers; paper; wood)	63.7	0.8	276.3	3.1
Clothing, footwear, leather and related products	221.6	8.1	541.7	12.5
Watches and jewellery	1 656.0	5.5	2 014.2	6.1
Electrical household appliances, electronic and telecommunications equipment	233.9	0.9	751.2	2.5
Machinery, industrial equipment; computers and peripheral equipment; ships and aircrafts	130.7	0.5	417.5	1.5
Household cultural and recreation goods; including toys and games, books and musical instruments	11.5	1.8	16.1	2.6
Total sales losses	**3 582.9**	**1.2**	**4 481.3**	**1.4**

Impact on jobs in the Swiss manufacturing industry

Lower sales in the manufacturing industry reduce the demand for labour and consequently lead to job losses. Prior to calculating the job losses for the manufacturing industry, the sales elasticity of employment was determined for each sector (see Table 1.2). These elasticities represent the extent to which each sector adjusts employment in response to changes in sales. The number of job losses, as well as the share of lost jobs within each sector, can be estimated by combining the industry-specific elasticities of employment with the estimated lost sales detailed in the previous section.

Table 2.5 presents the main results for several sectors of the Swiss manufacturing industry.

In 2018, the total estimated job losses due to trade in counterfeit goods infringing Swiss IPRs amounted to almost 11 000 people (or 1.7% of total Swiss manufacturing employment). Put it differently, these jobs would have existed in the absence of counterfeiting and damaging impact on sales. Unsurprisingly, the highest job losses due to counterfeiting were found in the watch and jewellery sector in absolute terms. This sector experienced the highest loss with more than 3 700 employees. It was followed by the clothing, footwear, leather and related products sector (around 1 600 people), and the textiles and other intermediate products and the electrical household appliances, electronic and telecommunication equipment sectors (around 1 500 people in each sector).

As a share of employees, the clothing, footwear, leather and related products sector and the watches and jewellery sector are also the most hit by the trade in counterfeit goods infringing Swiss IPRs since losses represented 22.7% and 6.7% of total sectors' employees respectively.

Table 2.5. Estimated job losses in Swiss manufacturing sectors, 2018

Sector	Jobs losses	Share of employees* (%)
Food, beverages and tobacco	1 054	1.2
Textiles and other intermediate products (e.g. plastics; rubbers; paper; wood)	1 452	1.5
Clothing, footwear, leather and related products	1 661	22.7
Watches and jewellery	3 786	6.7
Electrical household appliances, electronic and telecommunications equipment	1 477	2.0
Machinery, industrial equipment; computers and peripheral equipment; ships and aircrafts	1 210	1.1
Household cultural and recreation goods; including toys and games, books and musical instruments	18	1.0
Total manufacturing industry	**10 659**	**1.7**

* The share of employees is based on the number of employees in full-time equivalent positions as detailed in Eurostat's Annual Detailed Enterprise Statistics for Industry dataset, which may suffer from data shortage at the detailed level.

Impact on government revenue

Lower sales and lower profits for Swiss infringed rights holders mean they pay less CIT to the government. Furthermore, fewer jobs imply lower PIT revenues and lower SSC. Finally, lower sales on the Swiss domestic market reduce the VAT on consumption. However, one can note that only a tiny share of fake Swiss goods is consumed in Switzerland, most of these fakes being purchased abroad. An estimation of VAT losses is provided to illustrate what VAT losses could be at a country level. The foregone tax revenues due to counterfeiting amounted to almost CHF 124.3 million (USD 126.2 million) in 2016. PIT and SSC revenues experienced the highest loss at CHF 123.1 million (USD 125 million). If all the Swiss fakes were bought in Switzerland, this would lead to a VAT loss of almost CHF 190.6 million (USD 193.5 million).

In 2018, foregone revenues (labour income tax and CIT) due to infringement of Swiss IPRs amounted to CHF 157.5 million (USD 158.4 million). It represented less than 0.2% of these 2 tax revenues (Table 2.6.). If fake Swiss goods were bought in Switzerland, this would lead to CHF 263.4 million (USD 265 million) of VAT losses.

The foregone taxes revenues are in line with the low taxation profile of Switzerland. Indeed, in 2016, Switzerland ranked 29th out of 36th OECD member countries with a tax-to-gross domestic product (GDP) ratio of 27.8%. In 2019, the Swiss tax-to-GDP ratio (28.5%) was still lower than the OECD average (33.8% of GDP) according to OECD tax revenue statistics (OECD, 2020[14]). Nevertheless, the foregone CIT revenues may be underestimated since the data on the Swiss manufacturing margin are incomplete. Consequently, CIT losses must be interpreted carefully.

Table 2.6. Public revenue losses due to Swiss IPR infringements in global trade, 2018

Tax type	Value in USD million	Share of collected taxes (%)
PIT and SSC	157.8	0.26
CIT	0.555	0.002
Total	**158.4**	**0.19**

Note: PIT: Personal income tax; CIT: Corporate income tax; SSC: Social security contribution.
Due to margins data shortages, CIT losses are underestimated.

A similar exercise of quantifying the impacts of counterfeiting infringing residents' IPRs was carried out by the OECD for Italy, Sweden and the UK. These reports also rely on the same methodology developed in Chapter 1 and Annex A of the present study. In relative terms, the Swiss economy experienced sales and jobs losses lower than those of Italy. Indeed, the sales losses for the manufacturing industry due to counterfeiting of their residents' IPRs represented 3% of the Italian manufacturing industry's sales and job losses represented 2.3% of the total employees of the manufacturing industry. In terms of job losses, the UK has been less hit by infringements of their residents' IPR since job losses experienced by this country represented 1.3% of their employees. The Swiss government revenue losses were lower than Italian ones (1.8% of Italian collected taxes) due to its specific taxation profile while they were quite close to the UK ones (0.31%).

These comparisons must be interpreted carefully since the estimated losses for the Swiss economy rely on data that may suffer from shortages and are consequently underestimated.

References

OECD (2020), *Tax revenue (indicator)*, http://dx.doi.org/10.1787/d98b8cf5-en. [14]

OECD (2019), *Counterfeiting and Piracy and the Swedish Economy: Making Sure "Made in Sweden" Always Is, Illicit Trade*, OECD Publishing, Paris, https://doi.org/10.1787/eb300f5b-en. [13]

OECD (2018), *Trade in Counterfeit Goods and the Italian Economy: Protecting Italy's intellectual property, Illicit Trade*, OECD Publishing, Paris, https://doi.org/10.1787/9789264302426-en. [12]

OECD/EUIPO (2019), *Trends in Trade in Counterfeit and Pirated Goods*, Illicit Trade, OECD Publishing, Paris, https://doi.org/10.1787/g2g9f533-en. [11]

OECD/EUIPO (2017), Mapping the Real Routes of Trade in Fake Goods, OECD Publishing, Paris, https://doi.org/10.1787/9789264278349-en. [20]

OECD/EUIPO (2016), Trade in Counterfeit and Pirated Goods: Mapping the Economic Impact, OECD Publishing, Paris, http://dx.doi.org/10.1787/9789264252653-en. [7]

Notes

[1] OECD/EUIPO (2017[20]); OECD/EUIPO (2019[11]).

[2] Of course, many postal and express shipments arrive by air transport. However, customs offices in many economies distinguish between express/courier seizures (no matter what mode of transport), postal (no matter what mode of transport) and air transport (all seizures other than express and postal; for example, air cargo). However, for some economies, in particular non-OECD economies, there is no precise information on seizures of express and postal shipment; and all the seizures seem to be reported by the actual mode of transport.

[3] The indices included in the GTRIC matrix calculate the likelihood that a given type of counterfeit product of a brand or patent registered in Switzerland will be sold in a given destination economy.

3. Industry analysis

This chapter explores the trade in counterfeit goods infringing Swiss IPR in-depth for four affected Swiss sectors: watchmaking; mechanical, electrical engineering and metalworking industry; the FMCG sector; and the pharmaceutical industry. It provides an analysis at the industry level highlighting the most affected products, the provenance and destination as well as modes of transport used to send counterfeit goods infringing Swiss IPR. For each sector it also assesses the value of trade in fake Swiss goods and the detrimental impacts in terms of lost sales, lost jobs and tax revenues.

The watch industry

This section will focus exclusively on counterfeit watches (Harmonised System [HS] code 91). Importantly, watches are a vast majority of fakes in this category. Customs rarely report seizures of jewellery or watch parts (usually watch straps).

In 2016, the exports of the watchmaking industry represented 6.5% of total Swiss exports at CHF 19.5 billion (USD 19.8 billion) while they amounted to almost CHF 21.7 billion (USD 21.8 billion) in 2019, according to the United Nations (UN) trade database. In terms of value, Switzerland is the leading exporter of watches, far ahead of Hong Kong (China).

Asia accounted for more than half of Swiss watch exports (53%), followed by Europe (30%). The watch industry is particularly internationalised since exports represented 95% of total sales.

Figure 3.1. Main exporters of watches, USD billion, 2019

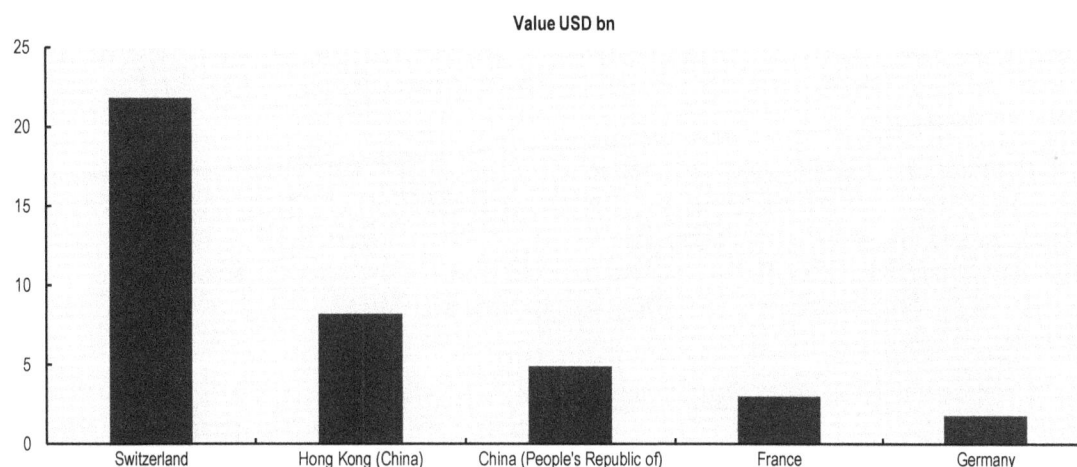

Source: *Fédération de l'industrie horlogère suisse FH*

Scope and volume of counterfeit Swiss watches

Globally, Switzerland suffers most from watch counterfeiting, since 55% of customs seizures of counterfeit watches concerned Swiss rights holders, well ahead of France, Italy, Japan, Luxembourg and the United States (US).

Box 3.1. The market for fake Swiss watches

The Swiss watch industry comprises a huge variety of famous and internationally known watch brands and has a unique tradition in watchmaking dating back centuries. Counterfeiting is a very big issue for the watchmaking industry due to the attractive quality and design of Swiss watches. The production of counterfeit watches and the intentional use of misleading geographical indications led Switzerland to protect its rights owners in 1971 by establishing an ordinance regulating the use of the word "Swiss" for watches.

The market for Swiss counterfeit watches is demand-driven. Counterfeiters react very quickly to changes in the demand for fake watches and have the capacity to adapt their offers on an industrial scale. The market for fakes seems to be segmented, with prices and quality varying from one country to another, correlated with the economic situation and income levels.

Fake watches are distributed all over the world, often in small parcels via certain national postal services or private delivery companies. The role and responsibility of such intermediaries in the supply chain are sometimes questionable, according to experts at the Federation of the Swiss Watch Industry (FH). Counterfeiters also use specific and strategically situated storage and transit hubs, for example the United Arab Emirates (UAE), to ship the watches to end consumers.

The use of the Internet for selling fake watches is not a new phenomenon and is increasing. Many online platforms (Alibaba, Bukalapak and others) and social media (such as Facebook Marketplace and WhatsApp) are used as distribution channels. Even YouTube is involved, since there are videos explaining how to buy fake watches, with links to sales websites. However, some Internet sales channels have taken active measures to prevent counterfeiters from easily posting fake products on their platforms.

The FH gathers more than 450 members from the watchmaking industry. Under the umbrella of its anti-counterfeiting group, the FH organises seizure operations and awareness-raising campaigns all over the world. As a result, the FH and its partners seize millions of fake watches every year and train hundreds of police and customs officers in the fight against the illegal phenomenon of fake watches. Together with its partners, the FH also intervenes in consultation procedures in order to improve the protection of its members' intellectual property rights (IPRs) and works to raise consumer awareness about both blatant counterfeiting and its hidden labyrinths.

The interviews with representatives of Swiss industries (see also Box 3.3 for an interview with the Swiss mechanical and electrical engineering [MEM] industries) have been designed to gather qualitative expertise about counterfeiting that we are not able to spot with our dataset. It is also important to note that customs authorities are not the sole data source for counterfeiting. As a result, the more global approach taken by the industries may highlight certain findings that are different from those based on our dataset on customs seizures.

Source: Interview with representatives from the Federation of the Swiss Watch Industry (FH).

The best estimates using the data provided by customs authorities and the General Trade-Related Index of Counterfeiting (GTRIC) methodology indicate that, in 2018, the global trade in counterfeit and pirated Swiss watches amounted to as much as CHF 3.35 billion (USD 3.37 billion) (Table 3.1.).

Table 3.1. Estimated value of global trade in counterfeit Swiss watches, 2018

	Value of fakes (USD billion)	Share of Swiss watches exports (%)
Ceiling value 20%	3.37	15.6
Ceiling value 15%	2.52	11.6
Ceiling value 10%	1.68	7.8

Trade routes

Over the 2011-16 period, the seized fake Swiss watches mainly came from Asia (China 53.3%, Hong Kong (China) 25.4%, Singapore 9.2% and Turkey 2.2%).

China and Hong Kong (China) were also the 2 main provenance countries in terms of seized value, respectively representing 67% and 22.4% of the value of seized counterfeit Swiss watches. They were followed by Malaysia (2.3%) and Morocco (1.6%).

Over the 2017-19 period, China and Hong Kong (China) remained the 2 main provenance economies for fake Swiss watches, representing respectively 53% and 24% of customs seizures (Figure 3.2). They were followed by Singapore, Turkey and Tuvalu.

Hong Kong (China) was the first provenance economy for fake Swiss watches whose share of seized value amounted to 84% (+59 percentage points compared to the previous period).

Figure 3.2. Top 15 provenance economies of counterfeit Swiss watches, 2017-19

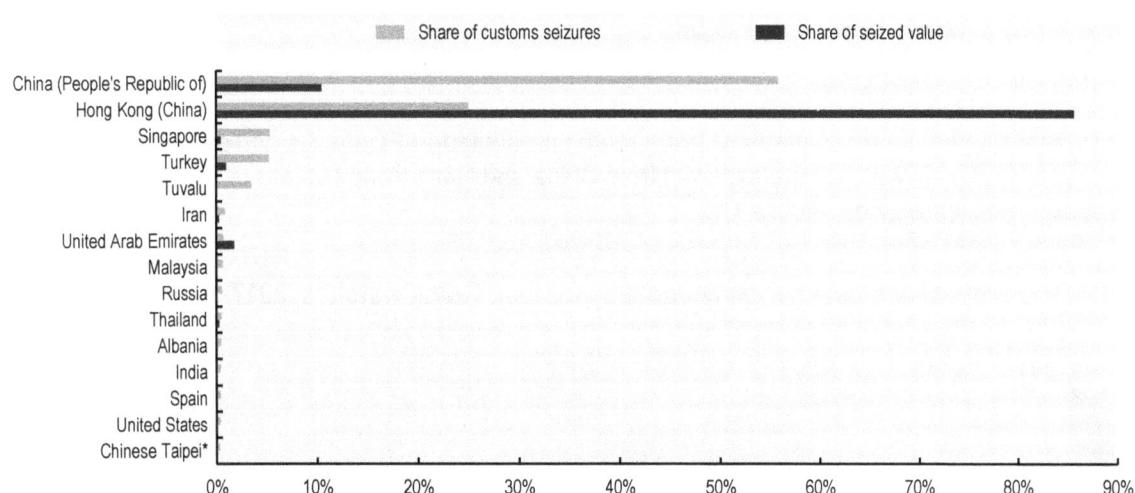

Note: The data from US customs are not included in this figure.
Tuvalu is a seasonal transit point, misused by traffickers in their operations.
Source: OECD customs seizures database

European countries were almost the only destination for counterfeit Swiss watches in terms of shares of customs seizures over the 2011-16 period. Together Belgium, Denmark, Germany, Italy and the United Kingdom (UK) represent more than 80% of customs seizures. In terms of seized value, however, the picture is quite different, with Spain, Germany, the United Kingdom, France and Argentina being the main destination countries for fake Swiss watches. The non-European countries appearing on the list of destination countries for seized value include Argentina, , Brazil, Nigeria, Uruguay and the US and Morocco. Together they represent around 13% of the total seized value.

Over 2017-2019, European countries were the main destination countries for fake Swiss watches. Germany, Belgium, the Netherlands and Spain being on the top of the destination countries' list (Figure 3.3).

In terms of seized value, United Kingdom is by far the first destination for fake Swiss watches (77% of seized value) followed by Germany, the Netherlands and Portugal.

Figure 3.3. Main destination economies for counterfeit Swiss watches, 2017-2019

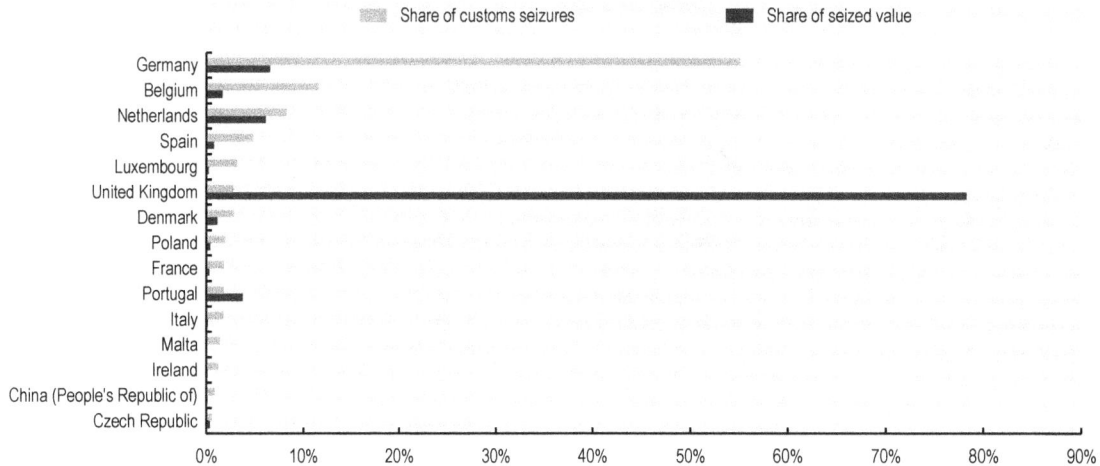

Note: The data from US customs are not included in this figure
Source: OECD customs seizures database

Descriptive statistics on the most intensive trade routes presented in Figure 3.4. indicate that the largest share of counterfeit Swiss watches are exported from China and Hong Kong (China) to European countries (e.g. Germany, the Netherlands and the UK).

Figure 3.4. Top provenance-destination economies for fake Swiss watches, 2017-19

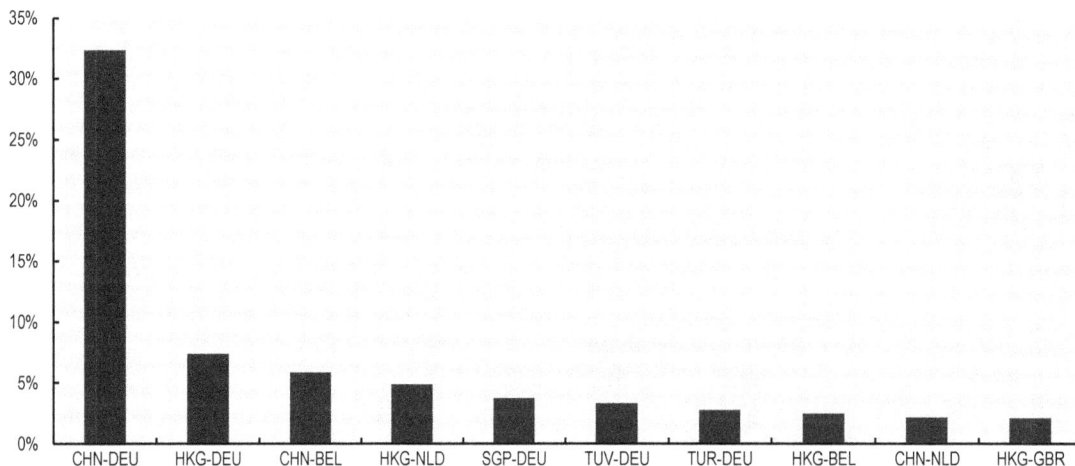

Note: These data come primarily from customs seizures data of the European Commission Directorate-General for Taxation and Customs Union (DG TAXUD) database, complemented by World Customs Organization (WCO) statistics. Consequently, the information for non-European destinations might be under-represented.
Source: OECD customs seizures database

Data on seizures also allow us to identify four countries that could potentially be transit points for counterfeit Swiss watches since they are both provenance and destination economies. These countries are Morocco, Kuwait, the United Arab Emirates and Greece. Greece appears to be a transit point for counterfeit Swiss watches. It receives fake watches from China, Turkey and Singapore and re-exports them to European countries (Germany, Italy and Malta). The transit status of the other three countries cannot be confirmed as data on production are not available.

Table 3.2. Potential key transit points for counterfeit watches, 2017-19

Provenance economy	Transit point	Destination	Transport mode from transit to destination
China (People's Republic of)		Senegal, Spain	Air
	Senegal**	Belgium	Postal
Senegal			
China (People's Republic of)		Germany, Portugal	Air
	United Arab Emirates**	Czech Republic, Germany	Express courier
United Arab Emirates (transit point)		Belgium, Ireland	Postal
China (People's Republic of)	Qatar**	Cyprus*, Denmark	Air
Hong Kong (China)		Germany	Postal

Note: *The information in this document with reference to "Cyprus" relates to the southern part of the Island. There is no single authority representing both Turkish and Greek Cypriot people on the Island. Turkey recognises the Turkish Republic of Northern Cyprus (TRNC). Until a lasting and equitable solution is found within the context of the UN, Turkey shall preserve its position concerning the "Cyprus issue".
The Republic of Cyprus is recognised by all members of the UN with the exception of Turkey. The information in this document relates to the area under the effective control of the Government of the Republic of Cyprus.
** Of course, it is highly possible that several transit points are misused on one trade route and that fake watches transit through Qatar and the United Arab Emirates on their way to the final destination. However, due to a shortage of data on production, it is very difficult to conclude with a high degree of robustness whether some of these economies (Qatar, Senegal and the United Arab Emirates) are producers or transit point.

Transport methods

As can be seen in Figure 3.5, methods used to transport counterfeit Swiss watches differ from region to region. Mail is the most common method used in Europe (53%) and North America (73%), while sea transport is often used in South America (41%) and Africa (62%). In all regions, air transport is the usual transport mode.

Over the 2017-19 period, mail (73%) was the preferred transport mode for counterfeit Swiss watches, followed by air transport (14%) and express courier (12%) (see Figure 3.6).

As a percentage of seized value, express couriers were the most used transport mode to ship fake Swiss watches.

Figure 3.5. Conveyance methods for counterfeit Swiss watches, by region, 2011-16

As a percentage of total seizures

Europe

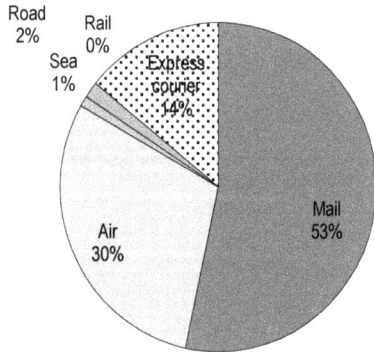

Road 2%
Rail 0%
Sea 1%
Express courier 14%
Mail 53%
Air 30%

Africa

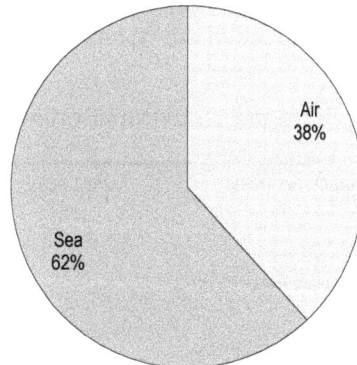

Air 38%
Sea 62%

Middle East

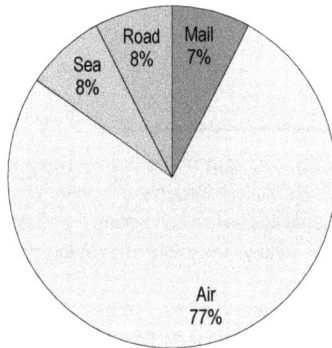

Mail 7%
Road 8%
Sea 8%
Air 77%

North America

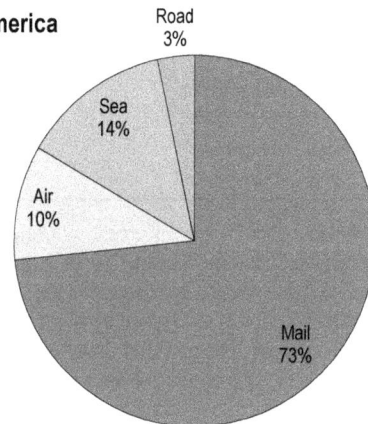

Road 3%
Sea 14%
Air 10%
Mail 73%

South America

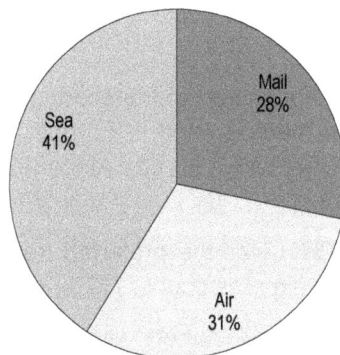

Mail 28%
Sea 41%
Air 31%

Note: Due to a lack of available information for Asia, transport modes used to ship fake Swiss watches to this region are not presented.
Source: OECD customs seizures database

Figure 3.6. Conveyance methods for counterfeit Swiss watches, 2017-19

As a percentage of total seizures   As a percentage of seized value

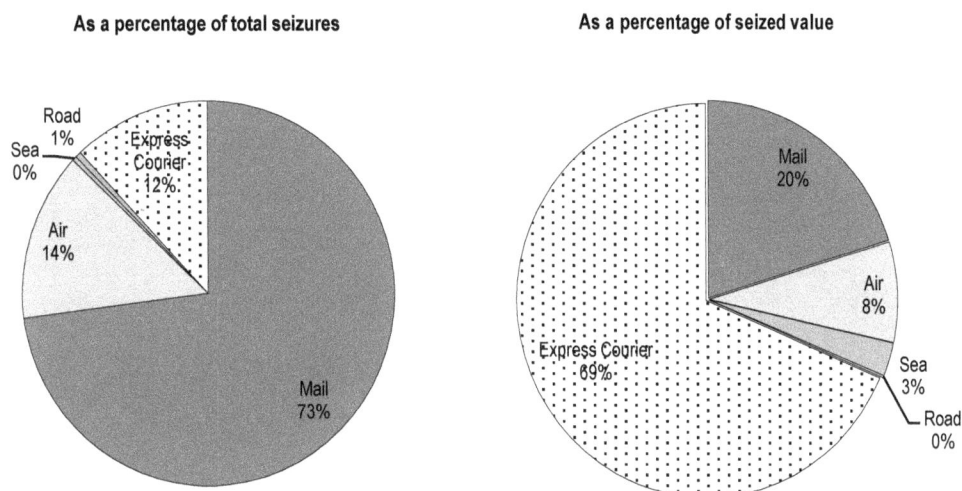

Source: OECD customs seizures database

Shipment sizes vary considerably depending on the region (Figure 3.7). Indeed, Swiss fake watches destined for the northern regions (Europe and North America) were mainly shipped in small parcels (i.e. fewer than six items), while those destined for southern regions (Africa, Asia, Middle East and South America) were shipped in big parcels (i.e. more than ten items).

Over the 2017-19 period, the size of shipment of fake Swiss watches tends to be smaller than in the previous period. Indeed, 94% of fake Swiss watches were sent in small shipments (i.e. less than 6 items) in 2017-19 (see Figure 3.8), while this share amounted to 91% over the previous period.

Figure 3.7. Shipment sizes for counterfeit Swiss watches by region, 2011-16

As a percentage of customs seizures

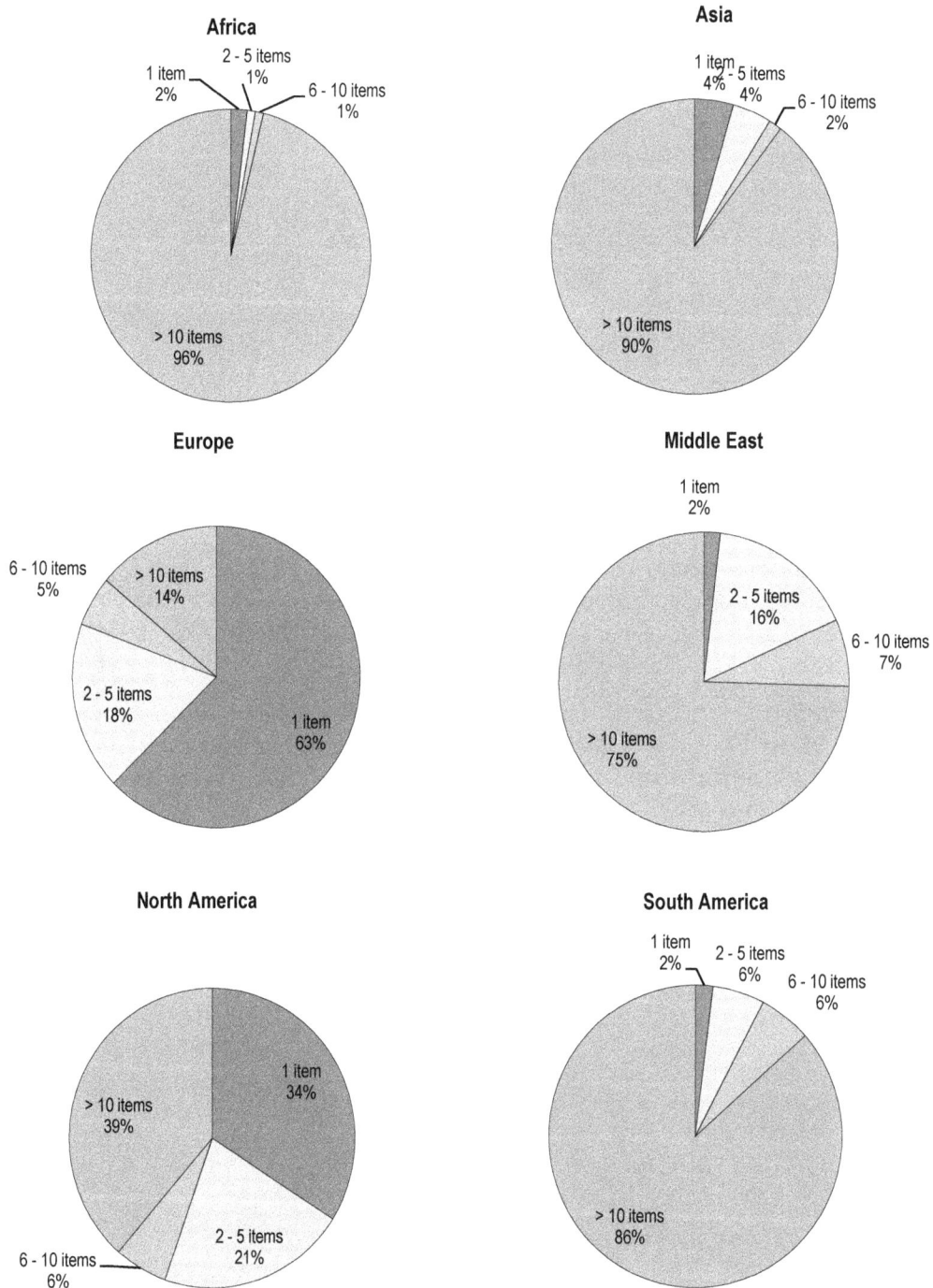

Africa

- 1 item 2%
- 2 - 5 items 1%
- 6 - 10 items 1%
- > 10 items 96%

Asia

- 1 item 4%
- 5 items 4%
- 6 - 10 items 2%
- > 10 items 90%

Europe

- 6 - 10 items 5%
- > 10 items 14%
- 2 - 5 items 18%
- 1 item 63%

Middle East

- 1 item 2%
- 2 - 5 items 16%
- 6 - 10 items 7%
- > 10 items 75%

North America

- 1 item 34%
- > 10 items 39%
- 2 - 5 items 21%
- 6 - 10 items 6%

South America

- 1 item 2%
- 2 - 5 items 6%
- 6 - 10 items 6%
- > 10 items 86%

Source: OECD customs seizures database

Figure 3.8. Shipment sizes for counterfeit Swiss watches, 2017-19

As a percentage of customs seizures

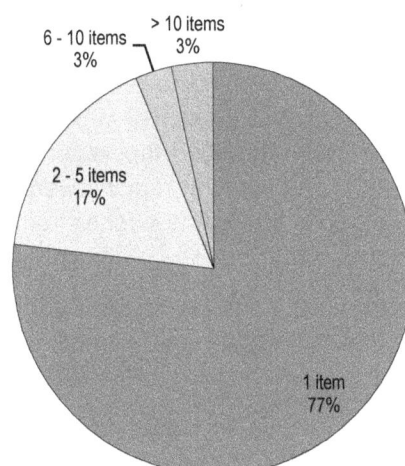

Source: OECD customs seizures database

The losses incurred by counterfeited watches

In 2016, the total value of fake Swiss watches traded amounted to CHF 2.67 billion (USD 2.71 billion). This implies sales losses of almost CHF 1.67 billion (USD 1.7 billion) for Swiss rights holders, i.e. more than 8.4% of the sector's exports, implying 3 000 lost jobs. Swiss watch rights holders are particularly targeted by counterfeiters and the whole industry is heavily hit by counterfeiting.

In 2018, the total value of fake Swiss watches amounted to CHF 3.35 billion (USD 3.37 billion), when calculating with the upper limit of counterfeit trade. This implies sales losses of almost CHF 1.98 billion (USD 2 billion) equivalent to 9.3% of the sector's exports and more than 3 700 job losses for Swiss watchmaking rights holders.

This massive counterfeiting of Swiss watches also implies damages in terms of government revenues.

In 2018, trade in counterfeit Swiss watches led to foregone revenues (labour income tax and corporate income tax [CIT]) of almost CHF 66.2 million (USD 66.6 million) for the Swiss government. If the fake Swiss watches were bought in Switzerland, this could represent an additional loss of CHF 154.1 million (USD 155 million) of value-added tax (VAT).

The large share of the secondary market for fake watches, estimated at 55% (Table 2.2.), reveals the strong demand for fake versions of Swiss watches (Box 3.1.). This means that more than 55% of fake watches have been sold to people who knew they were fakes. As for the primary market, where people buy fakes unknowingly, we estimate the consumer detriment due to counterfeiting to be almost CHF 1.78 billion (USD 1.79 billion).

COVID-19 crisis and trade in counterfeit Swiss watches

The ongoing COVID-19 pandemic has triggered a crisis that has had and will continue to have a significant impact on illicit trade in counterfeit goods in many sectors, including watches. The situation is dynamic and it is too early to conclude about the final, overall effect that the pandemic has had on the illicit trade in fake Swiss watches. However, dialogue with the enforcement officials, the industry and from ongoing reports permit us to draw some early conclusions.

As for the short-term effects, several COVID-19-related factors have shaped the landscape of illicit trade for fake Swiss watches. These include: i) heavy restrictions imposed on global transport; and ii) disruption in distribution chains due to lockdowns and health concerns.

Criminal networks have reacted very quickly to the crisis and adapted their strategies to take advantage of the shifting landscape. Counterfeiters have continued to supply counterfeit Swiss watches during the lockdowns in Europe and the US. This shows that these well-organised criminal networks have foreseen the disruptions of some transport routes and managed their operations accordingly. Of course, these criminal groups also benefitted because different world regions were not all affected by the pandemics simultaneously. Consequently, they were able draw some lessons from those regions hit first (e.g. far East Asia).

At the same time, COVID-19 also resulted in changes in customs control priorities (e.g. focus on COVID-19-related products) and labour shortages among law enforcement officials. Unfortunately, these factors reduce enforcement efforts to counter illicit trade in many counterfeit products, including watches.

Another observed trend is a substantial shift towards further misuse of the online environment. There is robust observable growth in the supply of fake Swiss watches on all types of online platforms, including those that used to be relatively free from this risk. In 2020, the Federation of the Swiss Watch Industry (FH) Internet Enforcement Team closed more than 1.2 million offers for fake watches on numerous Internet sales platforms.

To counter this quickly evolving risk, the FH has organised a set of online training courses for police and customs authorities worldwide. Also, support programmes for brand owners were initiated to offset the negative impacts caused by the illicit trade during the pandemic.

The mechanical, electrical engineering and metalworking (MEM) industry

The MEM industry is Switzerland's largest manufacturing industry, with the highest share of value-added according to Swissmem statistics. This industry includes the following sectors:

- manufacturing of basic metals
- manufacturing of fabricated metal products, except machinery and equipment
- manufacturing of computer, electronic and optical products (except watches)
- manufacturing of electrical equipment, manufacturing of machinery and equipment not elsewhere classified
- manufacturing of motor vehicles, trailers and semi-trailers
- manufacturing of other transport equipment
- manufacturing of medical and dental instruments and supplies and repair and installation of machinery and equipment.[1]

This industry is a pillar for the Swiss economy as it significantly contributes to Swiss sales, exports and employment. In 2016, the total sales of the MEM industry amounted to almost CHF 89.7 billion (USD 91 billion) in 2016 equivalent to almost 35% of all Swiss manufacturing sales.[2] In the same year, exports from the industry amounted to CHF 62.1 billion (USD 63 billion) which was 70% of the MEM industry's sales. The industry employed in 2016 around 317 000 people (full- and part-time), around 47% of all employment in Swiss manufacturing.

Despite the slowdown of sales of the MEM sector in 2019, it remained the first industrial sector in terms of value creation. Indeed, in 2019, this industry represented around 40% of the Swiss industrial added value according to the latest Swissmem statistics. In line with sales decline, the MEM sector's exports have decreased by 2.1% in 2019 amounting to CHF 68.3 billion (USD 68.7 billion). In 2019, the MEM industry remained the first employer of the Swiss manufacturing industry, employing 325 000 people (equivalent to 47% of Swiss manufacturing industry workers).

Scope and volume

Interviews with representatives from the MEM industry revealed that most counterfeit products are mass-produced items rather than large machinery (Box 3.3.). These products, such as pressure cookers, electricity meters, power switches and semiconductors, are relatively easy to reproduce in a way that could deceive potential consumers, without maintaining high quality standards.

In addition, counterfeiting in this industry also concerns falsified maintenance and machine safety certificates. Such fake certificates are used to deceive final users and convince them to pay a higher price for a substandard, counterfeit product.

As shown in Figure 3.9, during 2011-16, the sector of optical, photographic and medical apparatus and the sector of electrical engineering and electronics were the most impacted by counterfeiting in terms of both value and volume.

The targeted products of Swiss MEM counterfeits have changed compared to the previous period. Over the 2017-19 period, counterfeiters focused on electrical engineering and electronics, the most targeted products, followed by optical, photographic, medical apparatus and machinery and mechanical appliances (see Figure 3.10).

Electrical engineering and electronics products accounted for 96% of the seized value of counterfeit Swiss MEM products.

Figure 3.9. Seizures of counterfeit Swiss MEM products by HS codes, 2011-16

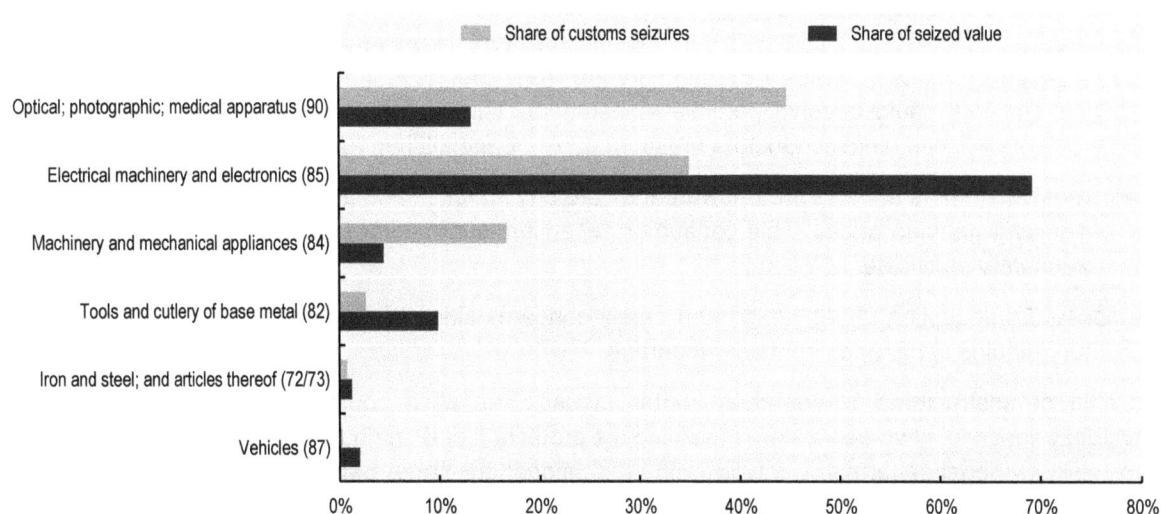

Note: The number in parenthesis refer to the HS codes corresponding to the selected sector.
Source: OECD customs seizures database

Figure 3.10. Seizures of counterfeit Swiss MEM products by HS codes, 2017-19

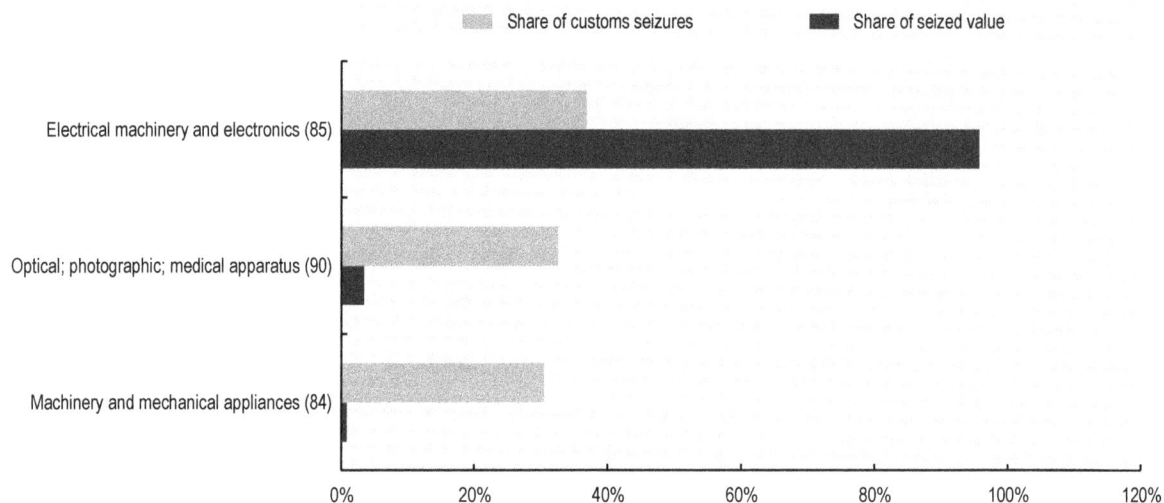

Note: The number in parenthesis refer to the HS codes corresponding to the selected sector.
Source: OECD customs seizures database

Box 3.2. Counterfeiting safety concerns and small- and medium-sized enterprise (SME) vulnerability in the MEM industry

The MEM industry is represented by the association Swissmem, which brings together around 1 200 companies. Most of these are SMEs and 90% of the business in this industry is based on business-to-business (B2B) relationships.

Industry delegates highlight that the range of counterfeits that hits the industry is very wide and includes such products as intellectual property (IP)-infringing escalators. However, in most cases, fake products that infringe the IP rights of Swiss MEM industry are mass-produced items that are relatively easy to reproduce and that could deceive potential consumers. This includes such products as electricity meters, power switches, semiconductors pressure cookers and kitchen appliances.

In fact, most customers of fakes are unaware they are buying fakes and are consequently deceived as they are paying genuine prices. This consumer deception is sometimes additionally reinforced by a counterfeit safety certificate.

The consumer deception raises health and safety concerns since the quality of counterfeit goods is lower than genuine items and could be dangerous.

The little or unstructured co-operation in this industry, as each company deals with this issue individually, leads to a two-tier system regarding the protection of IP infringement. While big companies have their own legal department or work with international law firms, SMEs face the cost barrier and cannot afford legal assistance to counter their IP rights infringement.

Source: Interview with a representative of the Swiss association of mechanical and electrical engineering industries, Swissmem.

The best estimates using the data provided by customs authorities and the GTRIC methodology indicate that in 2018, the estimated value of global trade in counterfeit Swiss MEM products amounted to CHF 1.89 billion (USD 1.9 billion).

Trade routes

Over the 2011-16 period, China (59%), Hong Kong (China) (30%), the UAE (1.7%) and Singapore (1.7%) are the main provenance countries for fake MEM products (Figure 3.11). They were followed by Thailand and Panama.

In terms of seized value, China is by far the most important provenance country of counterfeit Swiss MEM products, gathering almost 95% of the total seized value.

Over the 2017-19 period, fake Swiss MEM products originated from China and Hong Kong (China) (Figure 3.12). However, China has strengthened its position compared to the previous period accounting for 80% of total customs seizures and 96% of the total seized value.

Figure 3.11. Top provenance countries of counterfeit Swiss MEM products, 2011-16

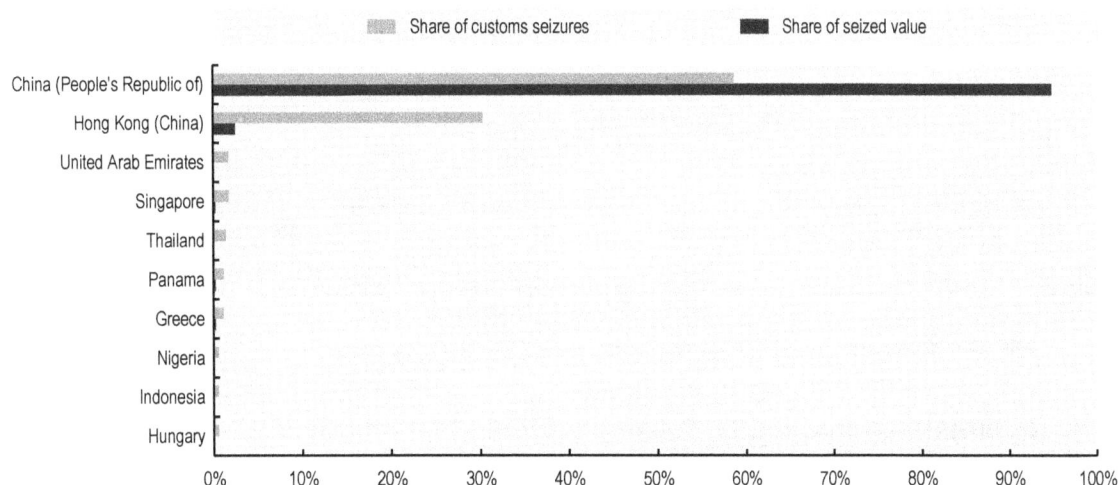

Source: OECD customs seizures database

Figure 3.12. Top provenance countries of counterfeit Swiss MEM products, 2017-19

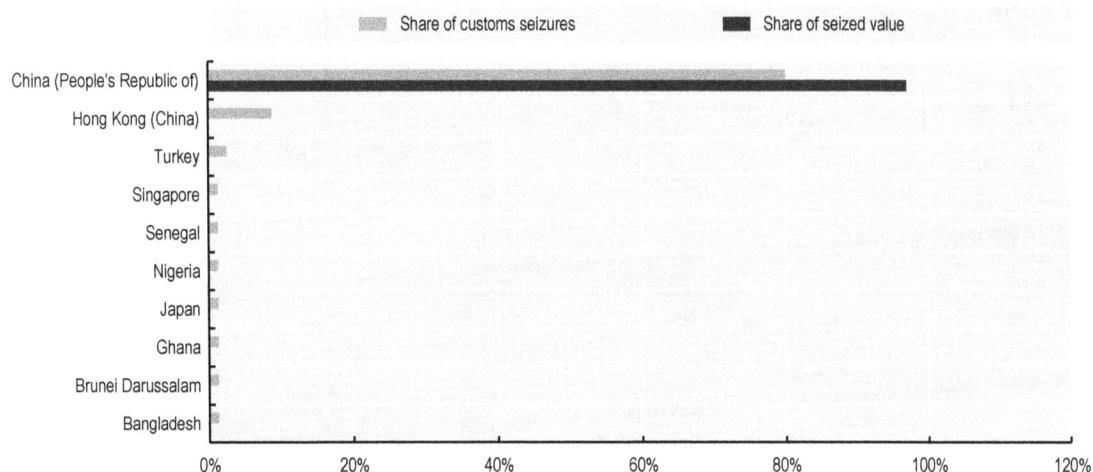

Source: OECD customs seizures database.

Figure 3.13 shows that Germany, Belgium, the US, Italy, France and Hungary (a provenance country as well) were the main destination countries for fake Swiss MEM products. Germany, Hungary and the US were the main destination countries in terms of seized value.

Over the 2017-19 period, counterfeit Swiss MEM products were mainly destined for Germany, which has strengthened its position in terms of both customs seizures and seized value compared to the previous period. It was followed by Belgium, Italy, the UK and Morocco (Figure 3.14).

Figure 3.13. Top destination countries for counterfeit Swiss MEM products, 2011-16

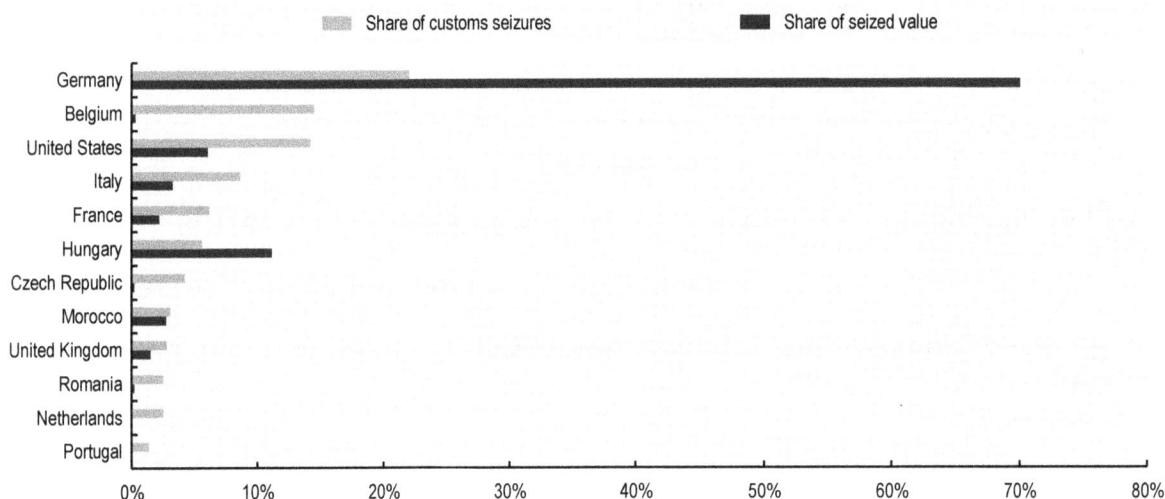

Note: The data received from the US customs are not included in this figure. Data related to the US come from the WCO customs seizures database.
Source: OECD customs seizures database.

Figure 3.14. Top destination countries for counterfeit Swiss MEM products, 2017-19

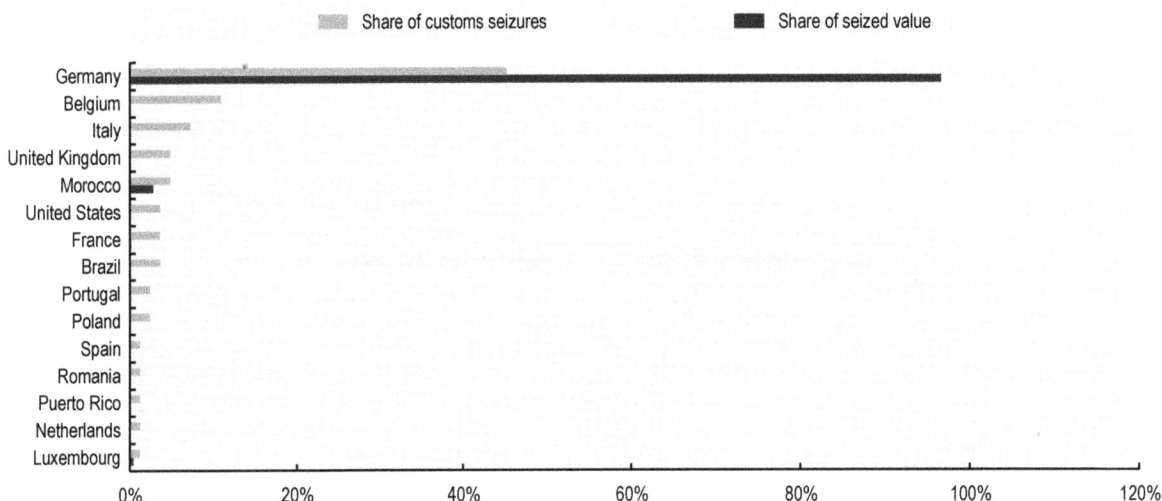

Source: OECD customs seizures database.

Figure 3.15 shows that regardless of the product category, China and Hong Kong (China) are always the top provenance economies. Apart from provenance countries that appear in other product categories (such as Singapore, Thailand and Turkey), Hungary and Uruguay are also on the list of main provenance countries for fake Swiss MEM products.

Importantly, for fake items from the sectors of "mechanical engineering" and "manufacture of basic metals and fabricated metal products", China was the origin of almost all fake products in terms of their value.

Over the 2017-19 period, China remained the main provenance country for all categories of fake Swiss MEM products. However, one can note the presence of unusual provenance countries like Japan being a source of counterfeit mechanical engineering.

Figure 3.15. Provenance economies of counterfeit Swiss MEM products, by product category, 2011-16 and 2017-19

Machinery and mechanical appliances (84)

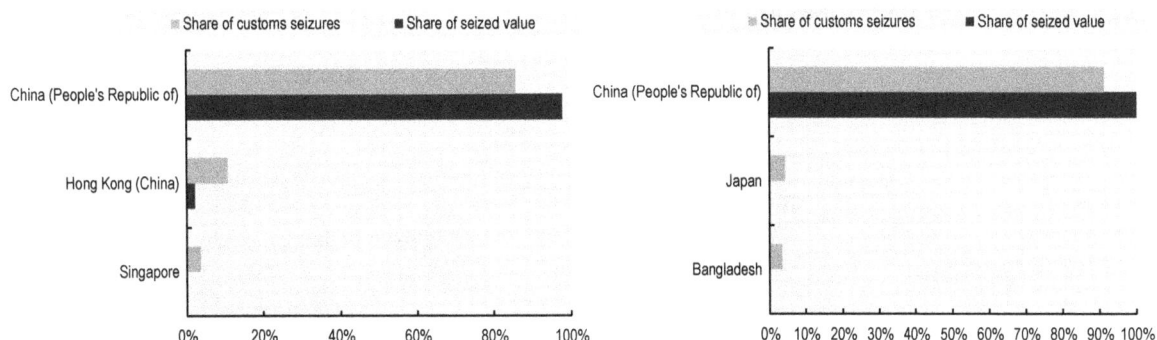

Electrical machinery and electronics (85)

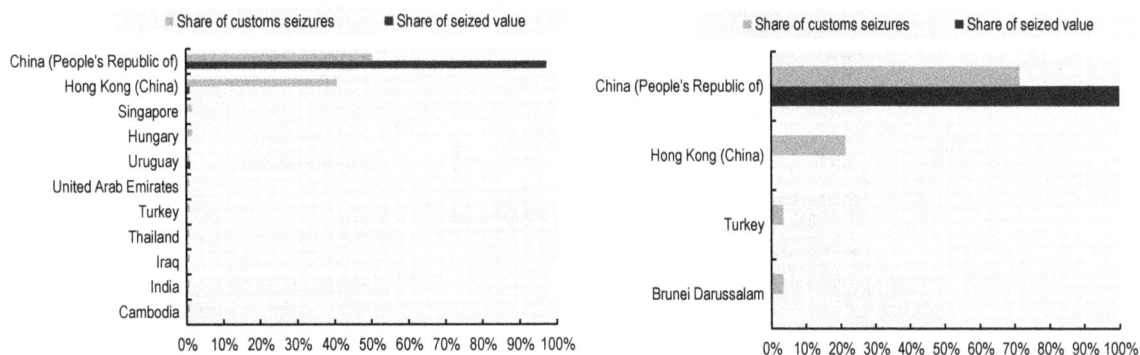

Optical; photographic; medical apparatus (90)

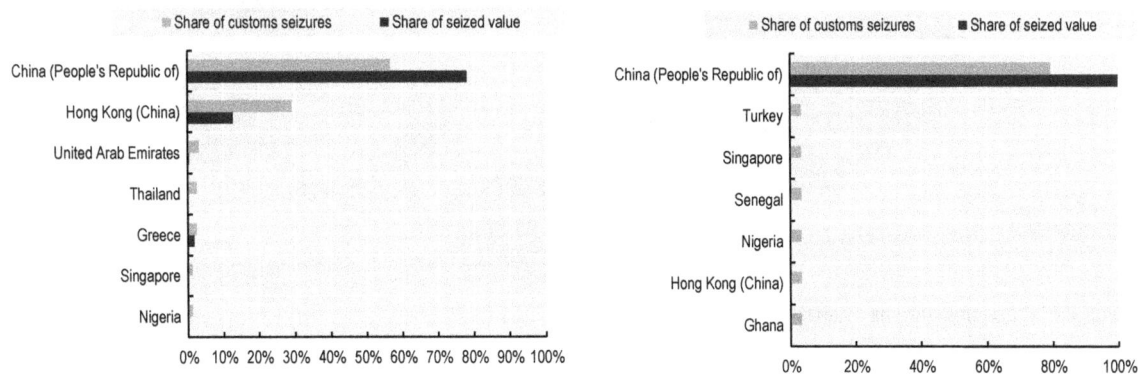

Source: OECD customs seizures database.

Transport methods

Over the 2011-16 period, air transport was the most popular way of transporting counterfeit Swiss MEM products to Europe, while sea transport is the most common route for products heading to South America. In both cases, mail was the second most popular method. These findings are quite in line with those highlighted in the watch industry section.

Over the 2017-19 period, air transport was again by far the preferred transport mode of counterfeit Swiss MEM products (representing 94% of customs seizures). In terms of seized value, fake Swiss MEM products were mostly shipped by mail and air transport.

Figure 3.16. Conveyance methods for counterfeit Swiss MEM products, by region, 2011-16

As a percentage of customs seizures

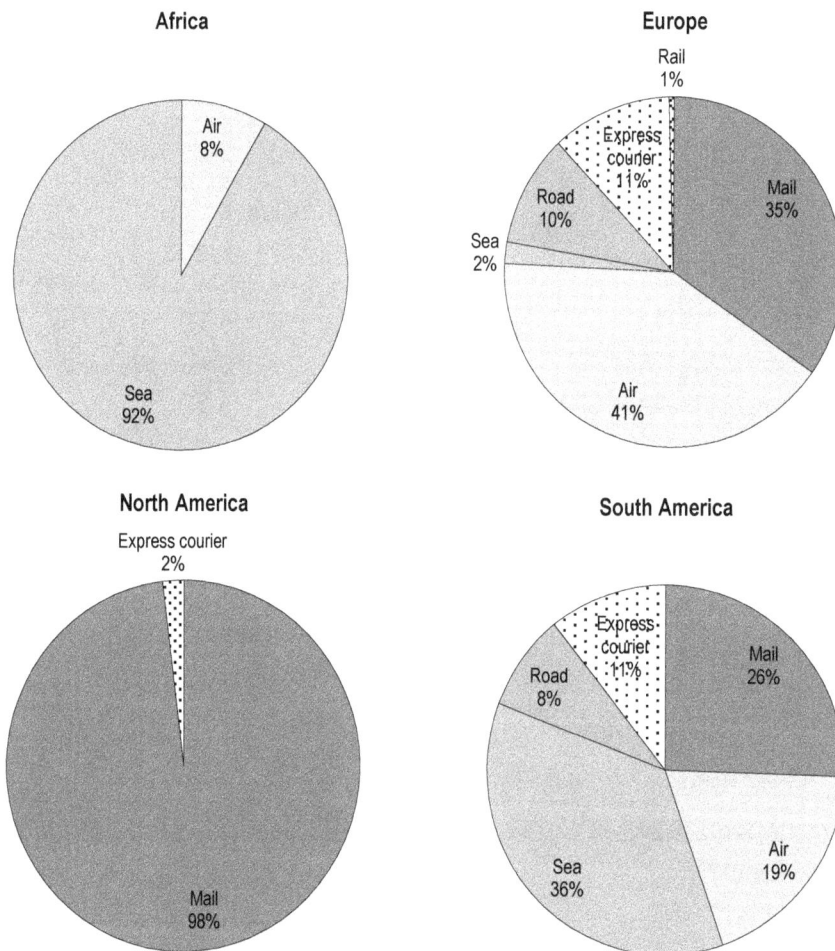

Africa

Air
8%

Sea
92%

Europe

Rail
1%

Express courier
11%

Road
10%

Sea
2%

Mail
35%

Air
41%

North America

Express courier
2%

Mail
98%

South America

Express courier
11%

Road
8%

Mail
26%

Sea
36%

Air
19%

Source: OECD customs seizures database.

Figure 3.17. Conveyance methods for counterfeit Swiss MEM products, 2017-19

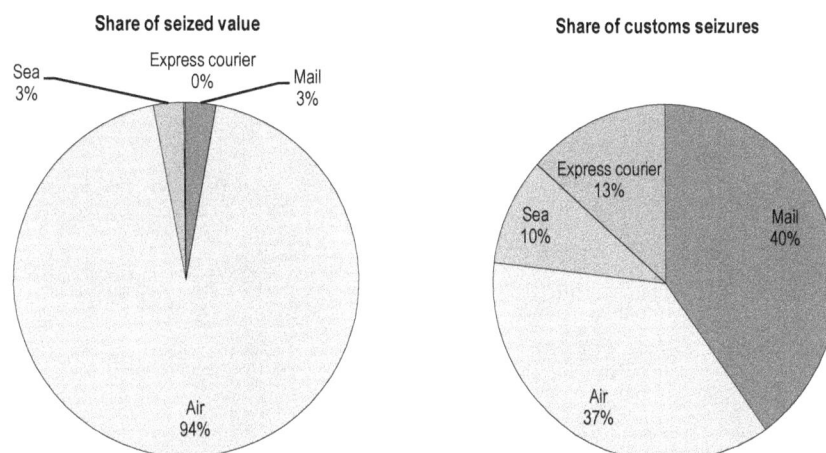

Share of seized value

Sea 3%
Express courier 0%
Mail 3%
Air 94%

Share of customs seizures

Express courier 13%
Sea 10%
Mail 40%
Air 37%

Source: OECD customs seizures database.

Regarding the sizes of shipment of counterfeit, MEM products, most of them were shipped in large quantities, with one shipment containing more than ten items. In the cases of the "mechanical engineering" and the "manufacture of basic metals and fabricated metal products" sectors, the share of large shipments, with more than 10 products in 1 shipment exceeded 60%, which suggest a particularly large commercial scale of counterfeiting in these sectors.

Over the 2017-19 period, large shipments (i.e. more than ten items) still dominated the trade in counterfeit MEM products. One should note that the shipment size of counterfeit Swiss optical, photographic and medical apparatus has varied over time. Indeed, in the recent period, small packages (i.e. 1 item) have increased, representing more than 40% of the customs seizures of this category.

Figure 3.18. Shipment sizes for counterfeit Swiss MEM products, 2011-16

As a share of customs seizures

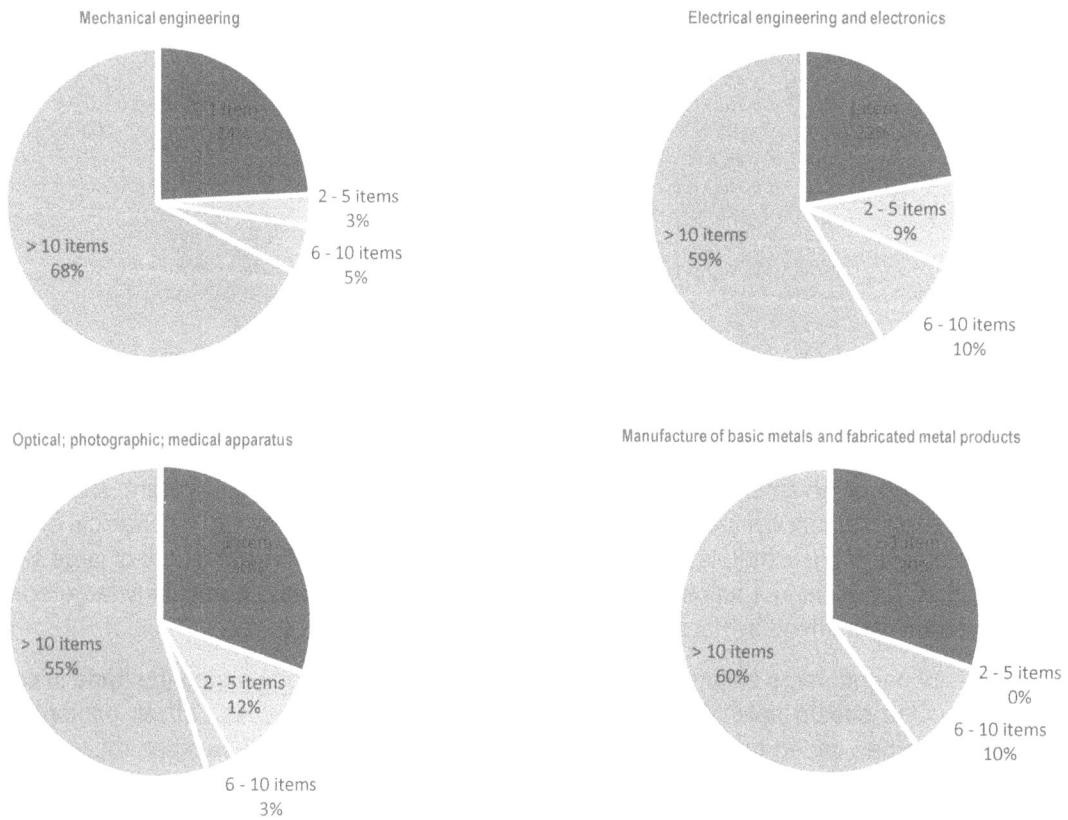

Mechanical engineering

> 10 items
68%

2 - 5 items
3%

6 - 10 items
5%

Electrical engineering and electronics

> 10 items
59%

2 - 5 items
9%

6 - 10 items
10%

Optical; photographic; medical apparatus

> 10 items
55%

2 - 5 items
12%

6 - 10 items
3%

Manufacture of basic metals and fabricated metal products

> 10 items
60%

2 - 5 items
0%

6 - 10 items
10%

Source: OECD customs seizures database.

Figure 3.19. Shipment sizes for counterfeit Swiss MEM, 2017-19

As a share of customs seizures

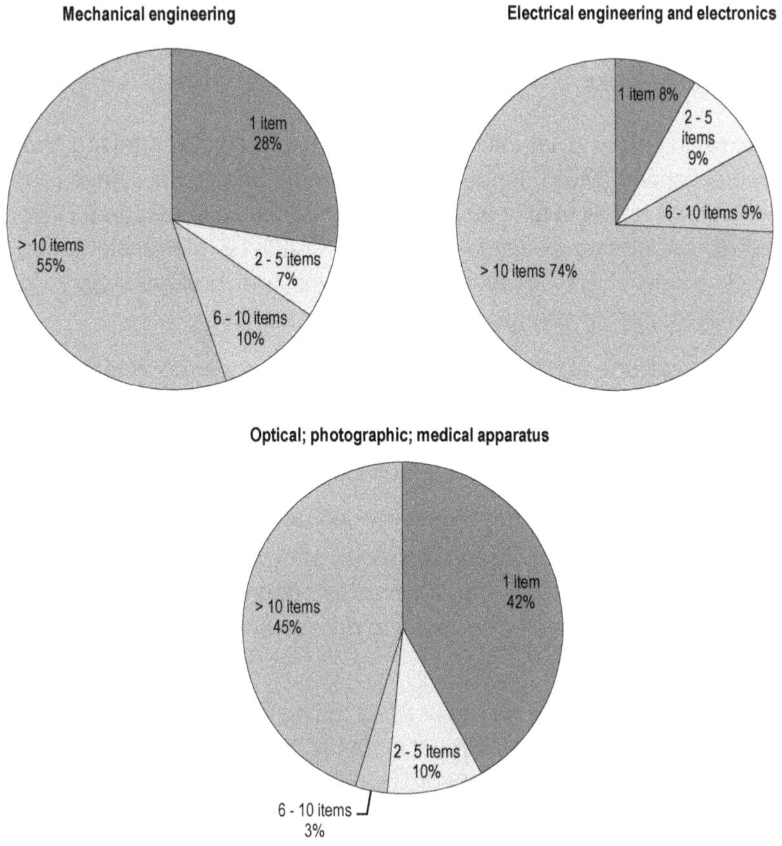

Source: OECD customs seizures database.

The losses incurred by counterfeiting electrical and mechanical engineering products

The sales losses in 2018 due to counterfeiting Swiss MEM products are estimated at CHF 1.16 billion (USD 1.17 billion) when calculating with the upper limit of counterfeit trade. In terms of employment, around 2 700 jobs are estimated to have been lost due to counterfeiting – about 0.8% of employment in the sector (Table 3.5).

In 2018, the Swiss government lost CHF 43.1 million (USD 43.4 million) of tax revenue due to trade in Swiss counterfeit MEM goods. Main tax losses came from foregone taxes on labour income.

Table 3.3. Estimated losses experienced by the Swiss MEM industry, in USD million, 2016-18

	2016	2018
Sales losses	364.6	1 168.7
Share of exports (%)	*0.6*	*1.7*
Job losses	1 002	2 687
Share of employees (%)	*0.3*	*0.8*
Tax losses	21.2	43.4

The losses experienced by this sector have considerably increased between 2016 and 2018. This trend may be explained by a change in customs profiling practices and the rise of the sector's exports between the two periods. Indeed, the exports of the Swiss MEM industry increased by 10.4% between 2016 and 2018 while the global Swiss exports rose by 2.9% during the period.

COVID-19 crisis and trade in counterfeit Swiss electrical and mechanical engineering products

The pandemic has reshaped and intensified the dynamics of counterfeiting the mechanical, electrical engineering and metalworking (MEM) industry sector. Criminal networks have reacted very quickly to the crisis and adapted their strategies to take advantage of the shifting landscape. Dialogues with enforcement officials and the industry delegates identified some key COVID-19-related elements, including: i) intensified misuse of the online environment because of lockdowns and broken supply chains; ii) change in the structure of trade in fakes; and iii) change in enforcement priorities.

There has been very intense use of the online environment, as under confinement consumers turn to online markets to fulfil their needs. For example, in the US, e-commerce activity has grown by 146% compared with the previous year. This resulted in a massive growth in the supply of all sorts of counterfeits on line.[3] For the MEM industry sector, an increase in the collection of fakes in all products was reported, including power switches and kitchen appliances.

The online boom also resulted in a considerable growth of new online marketplace and online platforms – created during the COVID crisis. The number of websites offering fake products of the MEM industry keeps growing. Apart from websites, criminals also begin to misuse new online channels of communication, such as WhatsApp or Facebook Messenger.

The industry continues to combat this scourge actively, using modern techniques, e.g. artificial intelligence. After detection, websites tend to reappear almost instantly, however. The effective prosecution of criminals behind these websites seems to be extremely difficult. Enforcement is also impacted by the pandemic and suffers from labour shortages. Besides, priorities have been shifting and anti-counterfeiting is no longer a prime concern. Also, changing trade routes in fake goods that infringe Swiss MEM industries also impede effective counteraction. According to the industry delegates' interviews, while production of fakes continues to centre in China, these goods are now transported with no logos to places closer to the destination markets, where the final assembly and counterfeiting act take place.

Finally, due to the pandemic, demand for personal protective equipment (PPE) grew sharply. This demand (for example masks, safety glasses, protective clothing) was sometimes not met due to closures of borders, distortions in supply chains or insufficient production capacities. Criminals entered this niche, not only offering fake PPE but also counterfeit Swiss equipment to produce PPE or spare machine parts. Such fakes cannot guarantee good quality PPE and could lead to significant health and safety risks.

The fast-moving consumer goods (FMCG) industry

The FMCG industry refers to HS codes 02/21 (foodstuffs), 22 (beverages) and 33 (perfumery and cosmetics). According to the UN trade database, the exports from this industry amounted to almost CHF 10.9 billion (USD 11.1 billion) in 2016, representing 3.6% of total Swiss exports. Sales from these 3 sectors represented around 14% of total sales by the Swiss manufacturing sector.[4] According to the Swiss Federal Statistical Office, this industry employed almost 94 000 people in 2016 (i.e. 11.5% of total employment of the Swiss manufacturing sector).[5]

Swiss FMCG industry exports have increased by 12.6% between 2016 and 2019. The value of these exports amounted to CHF 12.4 billion (USD 12.5 billion) in 2019 according to UN trade data. They represented 4% of total Swiss exports.

Scope and volume

Within the FMCG industry, the perfumery and cosmetics category is the most targeted by counterfeiters, representing 87% of fake Swiss FMCG customs seizures. This was followed by foodstuffs (10%). Counterfeiting of Swiss printed articles and beverages is quite anecdotal in terms of both customs seizures and seized value.

The counterfeit products in this industry that infringe Swiss IP are varied and include coffee, stock cubes, chocolate, soda, perfume, body care items and deodorants.

Box 3.3. Fake fast-moving consumer goods (FMCG)

Fake FMCG that infringe Swiss IP rights are mostly common consumer products such as foodstuffs (coffee, chocolate, powdered milk), perfumes and cosmetics (body care items and deodorants). For all these products, legitimate suppliers must comply with strict health, safety or environmental regulations to make sure their products will cause no harm or damage. In addition, transport and storage of legitimate products must also observe certain quality standards in order to preserve the high quality of these goods.

Counterfeiters do not observe any of these norms, neither for production nor for transport and storage. Consequently, fake FMCG are often of very low quality and can pose significant health and safety risks to consumers. Importantly, these health and safety risks also result in additional reputational risks for the industry, as well as the direct damaging effect of counterfeiting due to reduced demand for legitimate goods.

To counter these risks, the Swiss FMCG industry has been engaged in a number of awareness-raising and educational campaigns, highlighting the problem with consumers and pointing at easy ways of telling the difference between genuine and counterfeit products. Many of these campaigns and actions have been carried out regionally, to respond to local cases of influx of counterfeit goods on local markets.

Figure 3.20. Product category of fake Swiss FMCG, 2011-16

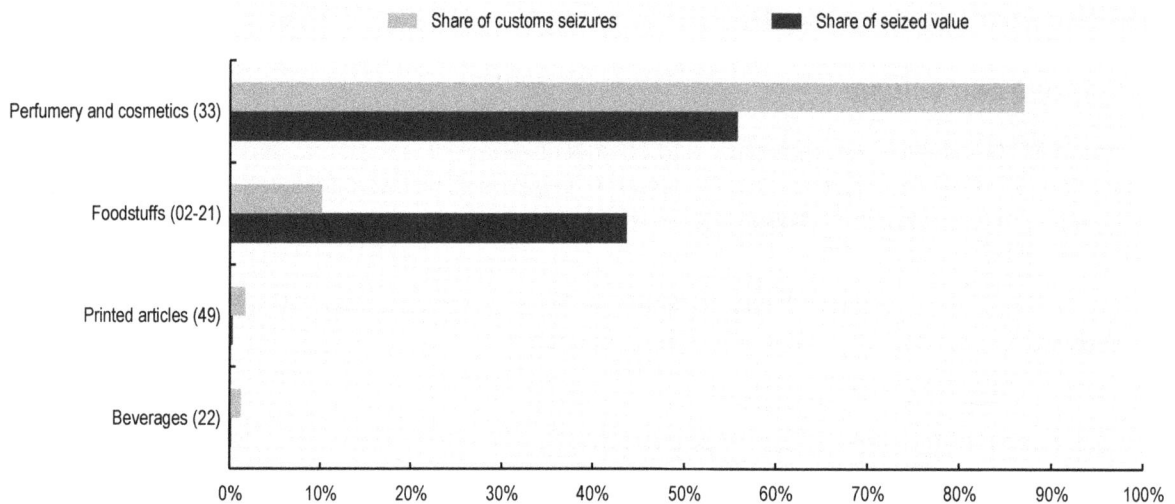

Source: OECD customs seizures database.

Figure 3.21. Product category of fake Swiss FMCG, 2017-19

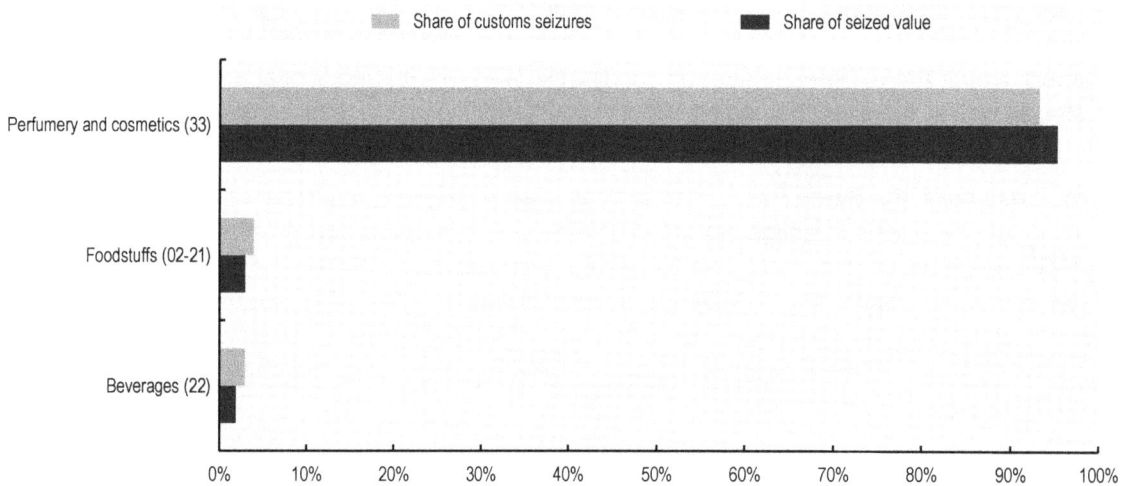

Source: OECD customs seizures database.

The best estimates using the data provided by customs authorities and the GTRIC methodology indicate that the global trade in counterfeit and pirated FMCG that infringe Swiss IP amounted to as much as CHF 198.8 million (USD 201.8 million) in 2016 (Table 3.4). In 2018, the value of fake FMCG was similar to the 2016 one, amounting to CHF 229.7 million (USD 231.1 million).

Table 3.4. Estimated value of fake Swiss FMCG, 2016 and 2018

	2016		2018	
	Value in USD million	Share of exports (%)	Value in USD million	Share of exports (%)
Ceiling value 20%	201.8	1.8	231.1	1.8
Ceiling value 15%	151.4	1.3	173.33	1.4
Ceiling value 10%	100.9	0.9	115.55	0.9

Trade routes

Figure 3.22 indicates that China and Turkey are the main provenance economies for counterfeit Swiss FMCG, representing respectively 36% and 30% of customs seizures over the period 2011-16. They were followed by the UAE, Singapore, Greece and Hong Kong (China).

Over the 2017-19 period, China, Turkey and the UAE remained the main provenance economies for counterfeit Swiss FMCG (Figure 3.23). However, one can note that China has strengthened its position. It is also important to highlight the presence of Switzerland on the list of the top provenance of fake Swiss goods while Switzerland is not a usual provenance country for these products. This specific trend is related to one seizure containing a large quantity of fake Swiss foodstuffs products coming from Switzerland and destined for Lithuania.

Figure 3.22. Top provenance economies for counterfeit Swiss FMCG, 2011-16

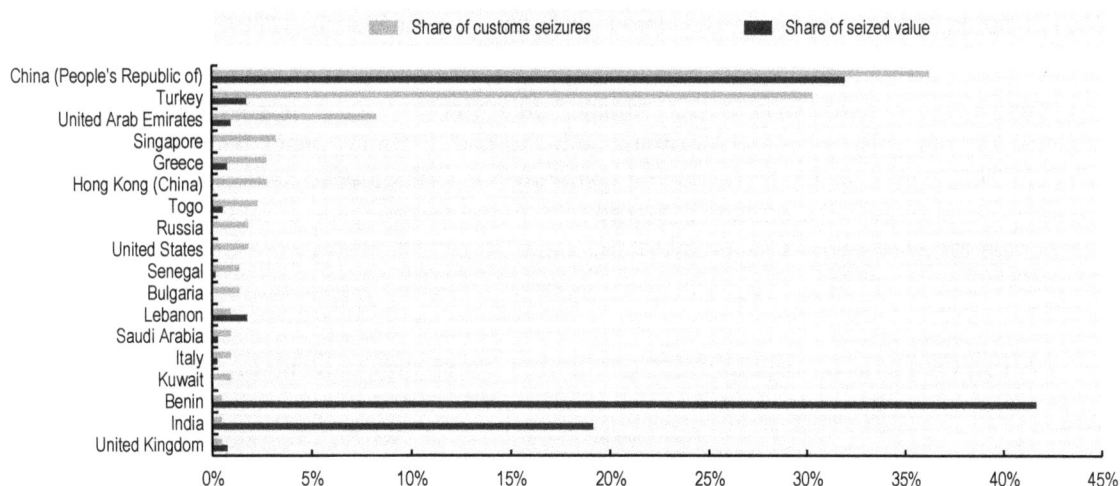

Source: OECD customs seizures database.

Figure 3.23. Top provenance economies for counterfeit Swiss FMCG, 2017-19

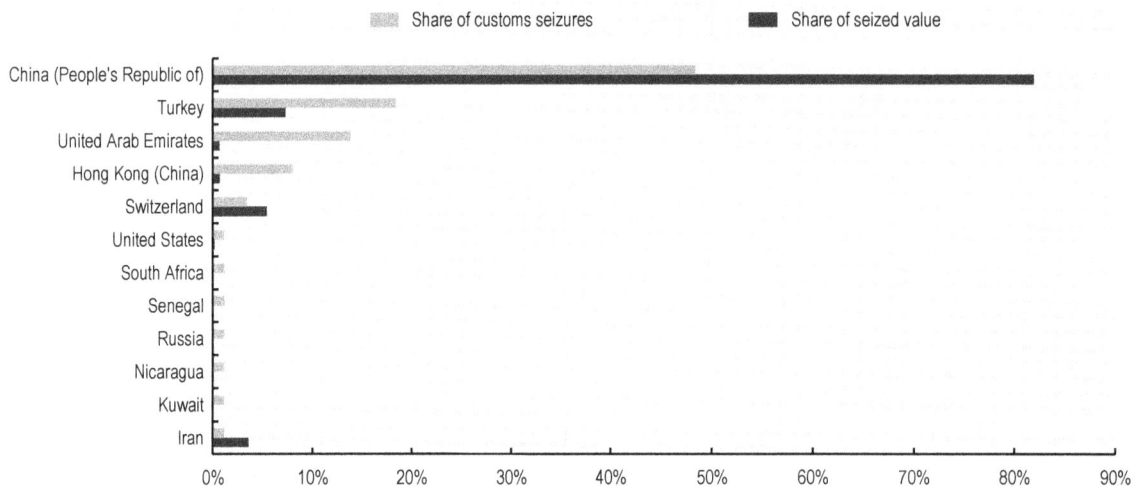

Source: OECD customs seizures database.

Over the 2011-16 period, the main destination economies for fake Swiss FMCG were European countries, led by Bulgaria (25.8% of customs seizures), Germany (18%) and the Czech Republic (8.8%) (Figure 3.24). They were also destined for African countries (Mozambique, Gabon, Tanzania and Morocco). Over the 2017-19 period, the fake Swiss FMCG were mainly destined for Germany (39%), Mozambique (13%), Belgium (10%) and Bulgaria (9%).

The main destinations of fake Swiss FMCG remained quite stable over the recent period compared to the previous one (Germany, Bulgaria and Mozambique being part of the five main destination economies for both periods). However, it should be noted that Germany has strengthened its position in terms of seized value. Over the former period, Germany gathered 13% of the seized value of fake FMCG while, in 2017-19, it accounted for almost 80% of the total seized value. It was followed by the UK (9%), Romania (7%) and Lithuania (2%).

Figure 3.24. Top destination economies for counterfeit Swiss FMCG, 2011-16

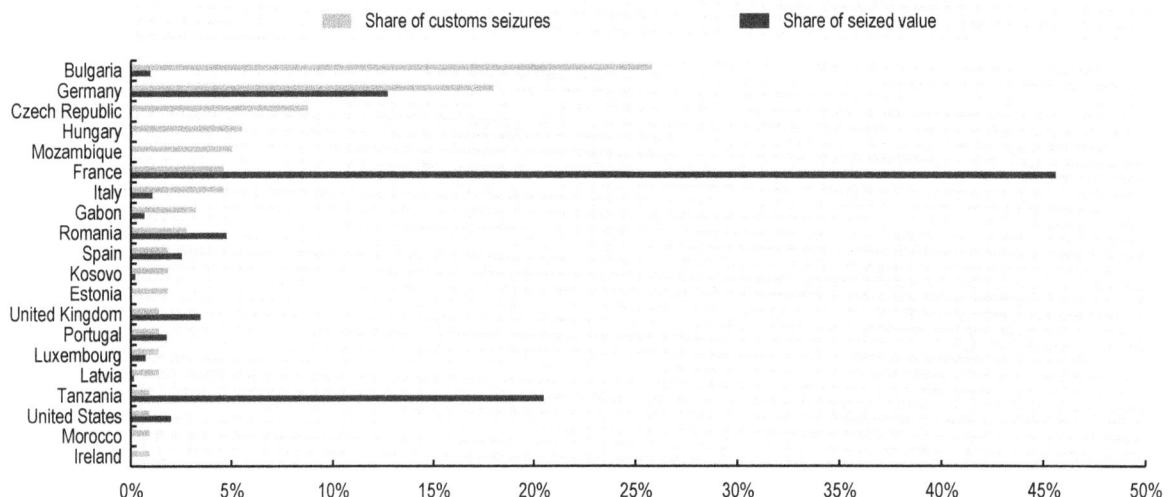

Source: OECD customs seizures database.

Figure 3.25. Top destination economies for counterfeit Swiss FMCG, 2017-19

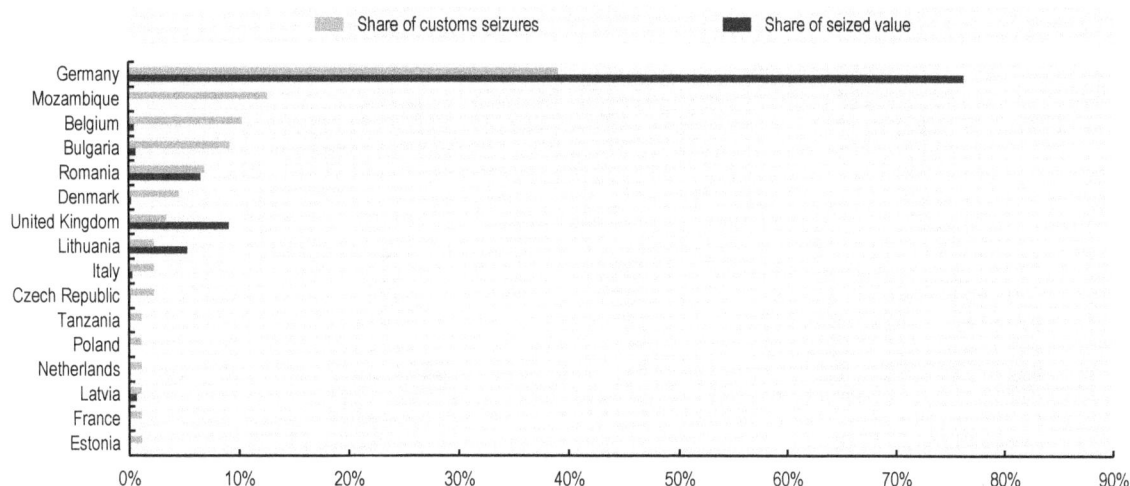

Source: OECD customs seizures database.

Figure 3.26 gives us a clearer picture of the trading routes for fake Swiss FMCG, notably showing the wide range of countries engaged in this counterfeiting trade. One can see: i) "traditional" flows, with fake products coming from Asia or Turkey and going to European countries; ii) the importance of African countries as both provenance and destination countries; and iii) "atypical" intra-African flows (fake products coming from Cameroon or Togo and going to Gabon).

Over the 2017-19 period, one can see that flows from Asia to European countries and from the UAE to Africa dominated the trade in counterfeit Swiss FMCG.

Figure 3.26. Top provenance-destination economies for fake Swiss FMCG, 2011-16

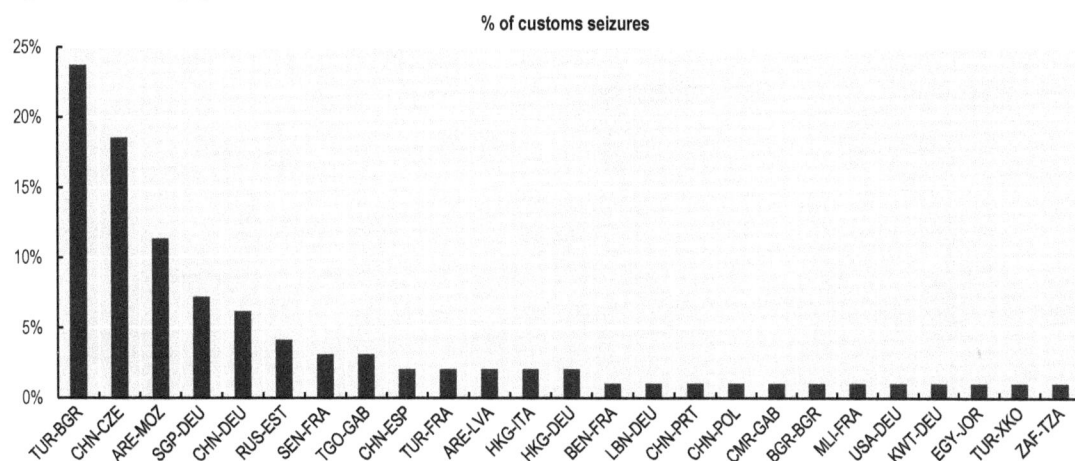

Source: OECD customs seizures database.

Figure 3.27. Top provenance-destination economies for fake Swiss FMCG, 2017-19

■ Share of customs seizures

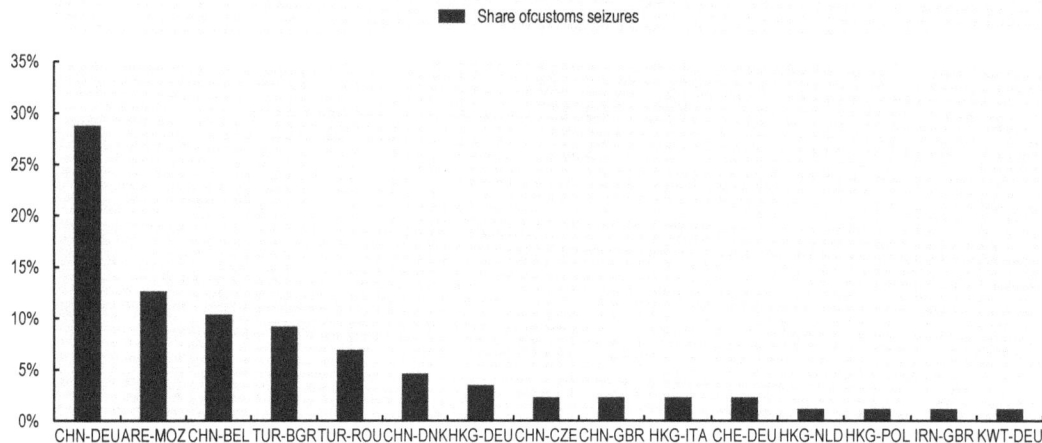

Source: OECD customs seizures database.

As shown in Figure 3.28, counterfeit Swiss perfume and cosmetics come mainly from China (39%,) Turkey (34%), the UAE (8%), Singapore (4%) and Hong Kong (China) (3%). In terms of seized value, the main provenance countries are China, Greece, India and Turkey.

Counterfeit Swiss foodstuffs, unlike other product categories, do not come from Asian countries. Instead, they mainly came from African countries (e.g. Togo, Senegal, South Africa, Mali and Cameroon) which represented 55% of customs seizures. Fake Swiss foodstuffs also come from the UAE and European countries (e.g. Greece, Italy and the UK).

Regarding the printed articles (e.g. calendars, booklets, notebooks) and beverages categories, the number of seizures is very limited (respectively four and three). The provenance economies for Swiss counterfeit beverages are unknown, while China is the exclusive provenance country for fake Swiss printed articles.

Over the recent period, China, Hong Kong (China), Singapore and Turkey remained the main sources of counterfeit Swiss FMCG. Provenance countries of fake Swiss foodstuffs have changed compared to 2011-16 since Switzerland is the main source of this product category. As mentioned previously, this is related to one big seizure of fake foodstuffs coming from Switzerland and destined for Lithuania. It was followed by Iran and African countries such as Senegal and South Africa.

Figure 3.28. Provenance country by product category, 2011-16

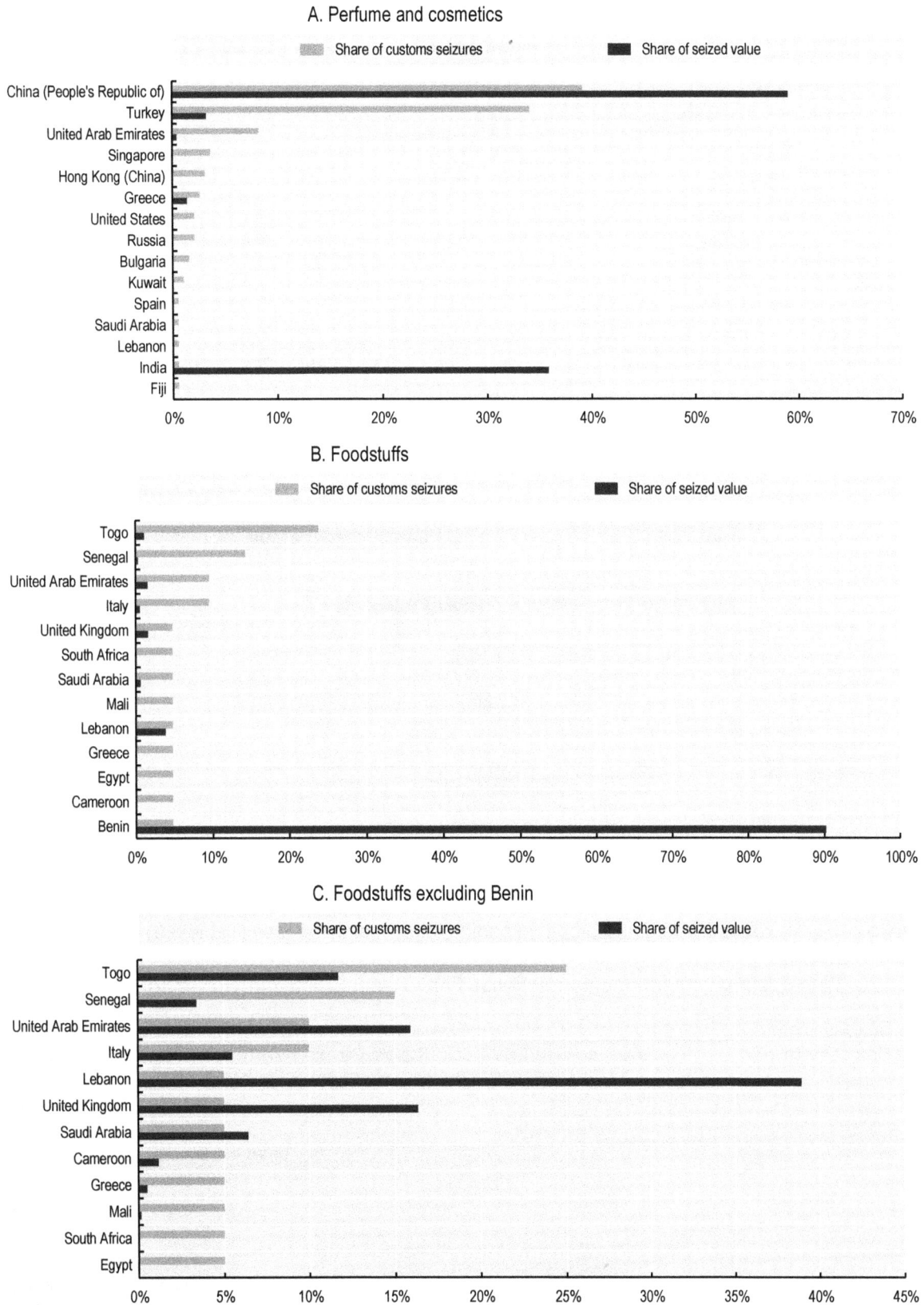

A. Perfume and cosmetics

Share of customs seizures   ■ Share of seized value

B. Foodstuffs

Share of customs seizures   ■ Share of seized value

C. Foodstuffs excluding Benin

Share of customs seizures   ■ Share of seized value

Source: OECD customs seizures database.

Figure 3.29. Provenance country by product category, 2017-19

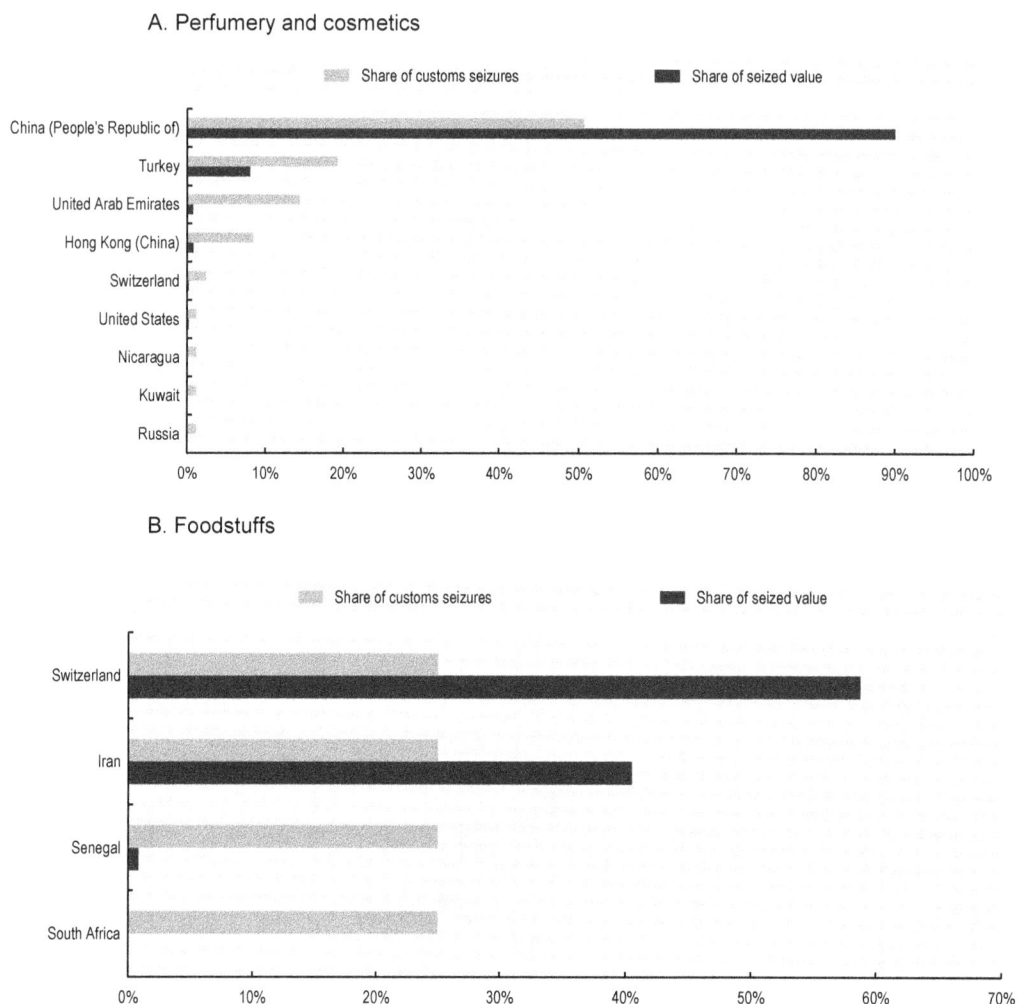

A. Perfumery and cosmetics

B. Foodstuffs

Source: OECD customs seizures database.

China and Turkey are indicated as the most important producing economies of counterfeit Swiss FMCG. While China targets many regions (Europe, the US as well as Africa and the Middle East), exporting fakes mainly by sea, Turkey solely targets Europe, exporting fakes mainly by road (Table 3.5).

Table 3.5. Main destinations for counterfeit Swiss FMCG from China and Turkey, 2011-16

Producing economy	Destinations	Transport mode
China (People's Republic of)	Europe (i.e. Austria, Croatia, Czech Republic, Germany, Hungary, Ireland, Italy, Kosovo, Luxembourg, Poland, Portugal, Romania, Spain, United Kingdom)	Mail - road - sea
	Morocco	Sea
	Saudi Arabia	Sea
	United Arab Emirates	Sea
	United States	Sea
Turkey	Bulgaria	Road
	Denmark	Air
	France	n.a.
	Germany	Air - mail
	Kosovo	Road
	Romania	Road

Table 3.6. Key transit points for counterfeit Swiss FMCG, 2011-16

Provenance economy	Transit point	Destination	Transport mode from transit to destination
China (People's Republic of)	Saudi Arabia	Hungary	Road
		Kuwait	
China (People's Republic of)	United Arab Emirates	Djibouti	Sea
		Guinea	
		Latvia	
		Luxembourg	
		Mozambique	
Bulgaria	Bulgaria	Bulgaria	Express courier
Greece		Italy	Road
Turkey			
Saudi Arabia	Kuwait*	Czech Republic	Air
		Germany	Mail
?	Russia*	Estonia	Road

Note: *In the dataset on customs seizures, Kuwait and Russia appear as both provenance and destination economies but their status as transit points is undetermined due to lack of data on production.
Source: UNIDO.

For both periods, the large majority of counterfeit Swiss FMCG has been purchased unknowingly (see Table 3.7). The secondary market shares of Swiss FMCG were lower in 2017-19 than in 2011-16, respectively 33% (45.8% in 2011-16) for the perfumery and cosmetics sector and 27% (37.4% in 2011-16) for the foodstuffs sector. It means that a lower share of these product types has been bought knowingly during the recent period. These relatively low shares of the secondary market are logical since fake FMCG could damage consumers' health.

Table 3.7. Share of secondary market of counterfeit Swiss FMCG

Product category	2011-16	2017-19
Foodstuffs (%)	45.8	33
Perfumery and cosmetics (%)	37.4	27

Note: Due to so few observations for beverages and printed articles, their share of the secondary market could not be determined.

Transport methods

Over the 2011-16 period, the counterfeit Swiss FMCG destined for European countries are mainly shipped by road and mail, while sea transport was mainly used for the rest of the world (Figure 3.30).

Over the 2017-19 period, counterfeit Swiss goods were mainly shipped by mail (50%), sea (22%) and road (17%). In terms of seized value, sea transport was the main transport mode accounting for 93% of the total seized value (Figure 3.31).

Figure 3.30. Transport methods for counterfeit Swiss FMCG, by region, 2011-16

As a percentage of customs seizures

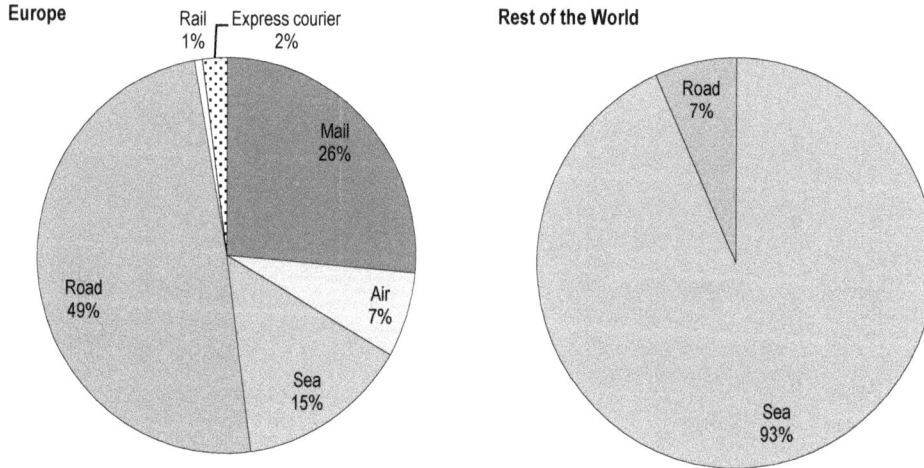

Source: OECD customs seizures database.

Figure 3.31. Transport methods for counterfeit Swiss FMC goods, 2017-19

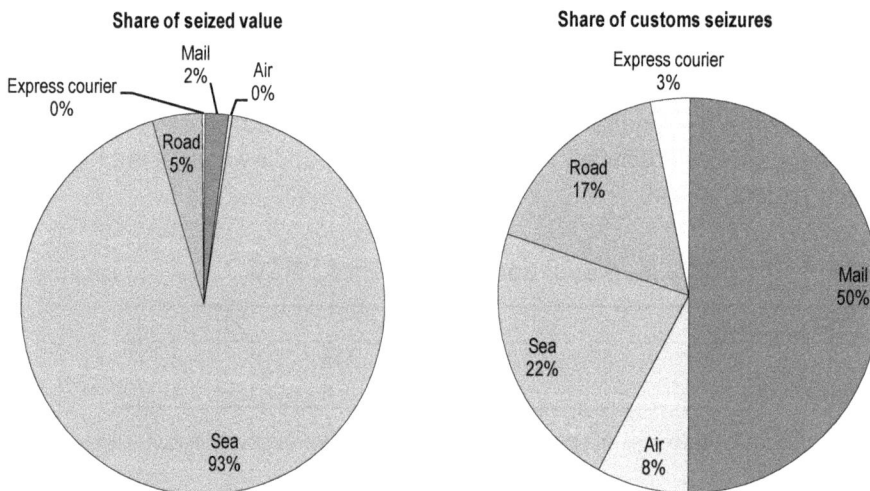

Source: OECD customs seizures database.

As indicated in Figure 3.32 and Figure 3.33, over the 2 periods, the counterfeit foodstuffs were shipped in big parcels: 100% of counterfeit foodstuffs were shipped in a parcel containing at least 60 items in 2011-16 (300 items for the 2017-19 period). Fifty-three percent of counterfeit perfumery and cosmetics was dispatched in big parcels (i.e. more than 10 items) in 2011-16 while this share amounted to 31% over the more recent period.

Figure 3.32. Shipment sizes of counterfeit Swiss FMCG, 2011-16

As a percentage of customs seizures

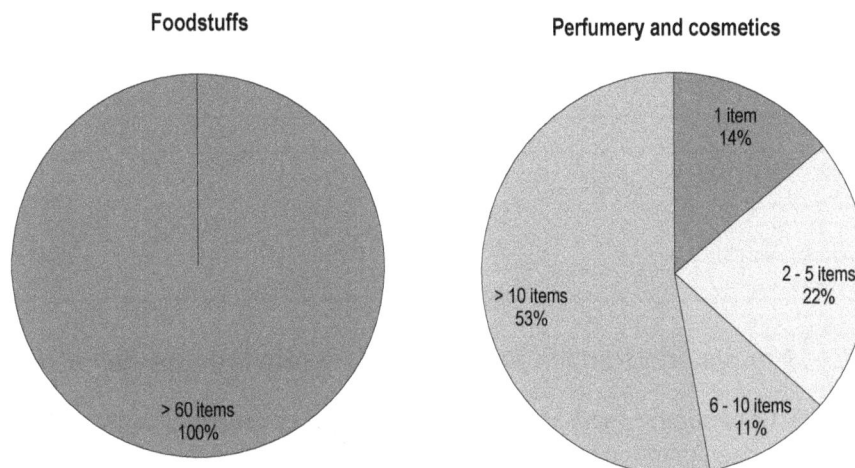

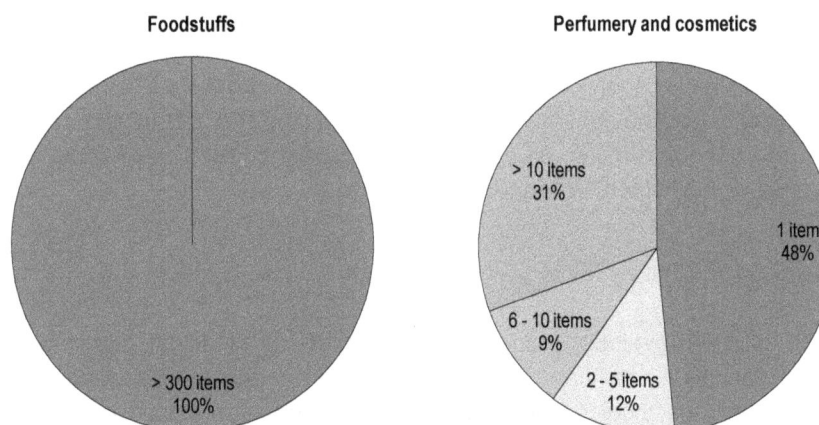

Foodstuffs

> 60 items
100%

Perfumery and cosmetics

1 item
14%

2 - 5 items
22%

6 - 10 items
11%

> 10 items
53%

Source: OECD customs seizures database.

Figure 3.33. Shipment sizes of counterfeit Swiss FMCG, 2017-19

As a percentage of customs seizures

Foodstuffs

> 300 items
100%

Perfumery and cosmetics

> 10 items
31%

1 item
48%

6 - 10 items
9%

2 - 5 items
12%

Source: OECD customs seizures database.

The losses incurred by counterfeiting fast-moving consumer goods

The sales losses due to counterfeiting of Swiss FMCG amounted to CHF 159.6 million (USD 160.6 million) in 2016, representing almost 1.5% of exports by the industry. It also led to job losses of almost 325 people or less than 0.4% of employment in the sector. Lost labour and corporate income tax revenues due to trade in counterfeit FMCG represented CHF 4.93 million (USD 5 million).

In 2018, the sales losses experienced by the Swiss FMCG industry amounted to CHF 189.6 million (USD 190.7 million), a level slightly higher compared to 2016. The job losses for the Swiss FMCG industry amounted to 250 jobs. The same year, the Swiss government lost almost USD 4 million (CHE 3.98 million) of labour and CIT revenue due to trade in counterfeit FMCG.

Table 3.8. Estimated losses experienced by the FMCG industry, 2016-18

	2016	2018
Sales losses (USD million)	160.6	190.7
Share of exports (%)	*1.45*	*1.53*
Job losses	324	242
Share of sector's employment (%)	*<0.4*	*<0.3*
Tax losses (USD million)	5	4

COVID-19 crisis and trade in fake Swiss fast-moving consumer goods

During the COVID-19 pandemic, additional fake fast-moving consumer goods, including those infringing Swiss IP rights, have been entering the markets. Closures of some businesses and disruptions in transport methods have led to significant distortions in supply chains. In all these cases, criminals leveraged these opportunities for illicit profits.

Due to the lockdowns in many countries, the online environment has become more intensely used, as the overall rate of digitisation has skyrocketed. It also resulted in a massive growth of trade of fake FMCG that abuse Swiss IP. The intensity of misuse of the online environment keeps growing and fakes tend to be found to a growing extent on new online sites and platforms, including social media platforms. In addition, enforcement authorities reported a significant growth in seizures of illicit food products (including illicit FMCG with Swiss brands) that had expired or where the expiry dates had been altered.

Furthermore, the dramatic growth in demand for PPE such as gloves or sanitisers resulted in a sharp increase in the supply of counterfeits in this area. To enhance their attractiveness, criminals tend to misuse existing trademarks of trusted companies, including Swiss FMCG producers. Counterfeits tend to put their brands on fake PPE, even when the right holder does not supply the PPE of this particular kind. This clearly illustrates the free-riding of counterfeiters on the goodwill established by Swiss FMCG companies and the trust that consumers associate with their brands.

The pharmaceutical industry

The pharmaceutical industry develops, produces and markets all kinds of medicine for therapeutic or prophylactic uses, vaccines, medicine for veterinary use, gauze, bandages, etc. and waste pharmaceuticals. This includes medicine whether or not in measured doses or packed for retail sale. However, this category does not include medical equipment, food supplements, dietetic or diabetic foods, mineral waters, etc. In international trade, pharmaceuticals come under the HS 30 product category.

Pharmaceutical industry – A particular context

There are at least four aspects that make the pharmaceutical industry particular in the context of counterfeiting:

- high IP intensity
- broad spectrum and notions of illicit medicines, including counterfeit, falsified, etc.
- particularly high health and safety risks related to counterfeit pharmaceuticals, in addition to socio-economic threats

- data-related challenges.

The high IP intensity

The pharmaceutical industry is particularly IP intensive. According to data provided by the World Intellectual Property Organization (WIPO), the pharmaceutical industry was the fourth most intensive in terms of trademark application, representing 7% of all world trademark applications.

This high IP intensity makes the pharmaceutical industry particularly vulnerable to the counterfeiting threat. This is confirmed by the available data. Between 2014 and 2016, the 2019 OECD/EUIPO report indicates that, based on customs seizures, of 97 recorded product categories, pharmaceuticals were the 10th most counterfeited type of product (2019[11]).

Switzerland being the second-largest world pharmaceuticals exporter,[6] is clearly a target for counterfeiters. Moreover, F. Hoffmann-La Roche and Novartis, two Swiss pharmaceutical firms ranked respectively 5th and 10th out of 21 pharmaceutical firms in terms of share of R&D expenditures to sales.[7]

Scope of infringements

There are many types of illicit pharmaceuticals and it is important to clarify what is exactly meant by the term "counterfeit pharmaceuticals" (see Box 3.4.).

As in previous OECD studies on trade in counterfeit goods, including the OECD/EUIPO study on illicit trade in counterfeit medicines (OECD/EUIPO, 2020[15]) this study generally uses the term counterfeit (or fake) pharmaceuticals or medicines referring to traded medicines that infringe trademarks. In this context, it stays in line with the definition used by the World Trade Organization's Agreement on Trade-Related Aspects of Intellectual Property Rights (WTO TRIPS). It also parallels the approach taken by the World Health Organization (WHO), in which counterfeit pharmaceuticals are described as "[…] deliberately and fraudulently mislabelled with respect to identity and/or source" (1999).

In addition to these discussions, many existing reports also include stolen and diverted pharmaceuticals (Box 3.4.). The existing datasets rely on largely incompatible and different methodologies and taxonomies and, in some cases, they also include stolen and diverted goods. Importantly, stolen and diverted goods enter the market without the consent of IP right owners and, in many instances, they also deceive final consumers. Hence, in many aspects, they closely resemble those counterfeit goods, produced without the consent of the IP right owner.

In addition, due to data limitations, this study does not look at potential or actual patent infringements.

Last, it should be also reiterated that this study is not intended to constitute any sort of new definition of counterfeit pharmaceuticals.

Box 3.4. Illicit, falsified, substandard, diverted or counterfeit pharmaceuticals

There are many, often overlapping notions of illicit, falsified, substandard or counterfeit pharmaceuticals that has been debated many times at several international fora. In particular, these issues have been closely addressed at the WTO and WHO.

At the WTO, the TRIPS Council took the IPR-perspective. The council discussed the negative economic impact that **counterfeiting** (i.e. trademark infringement) could have on economies, as well as the threats that counterfeit products could pose to health and safety. During the discussions, countries noted the distinction between IPR infringement and substandard products, as IP enforcement alone could not guarantee quality products.

In 2017, citing the confusion surrounding substandard and falsified products and the protection of IPRs, the WHO adopted new definitions (2017a and b) that are used in parallel to the notion of counterfeit (trademark-infringing) medicines. The new definitions refer to products which are either:

- **Substandard** ("out of specification"): Authorised medical products that fail to meet either their quality standards or specifications, or both.
- **Unregistered/unlicensed**: Medical products that have not undergone evaluation and/or approval by the national or regional regulatory authority for the market in which they are marketed/distributed or used, subject to permitted conditions under national or regional regulation and legislation.
- **Falsified**: Medical products that deliberately/fraudulently misrepresent their identity, composition or source.

Another category of illicit pharmaceuticals that is often present in the debate is **diverted** pharmaceuticals. According to the Pharmaceutical Security Institute (PSI, 2019[16]), such illegal diversion occurs when a genuine pharmaceutical product is approved and intended for sale in one country but is then illegally intercepted and sold in another. At times, drug regulators in the second country have not approved the use of the diverted drug.

A similar phenomenon is pharmaceutical theft, defined as the illegal taking of medicines (PSI, 2019[16]). **Stolen** pharmaceuticals can enter illicit markets through burglary, robbery or the embezzlement of goods, anywhere in the distribution chain such as at the site of manufacture, freight forwarder, distribution centres, warehouses, pharmacies or hospitals.

Importantly, as with classical cases of counterfeiting, diverted and stolen pharmaceuticals escape the control of the IP right owner. Moreover, these medicines are unlawfully supplied to the public, often without observing prescription conditions. Consequently, diverted and stolen drugs in most cases can potentially be damaging to consumers' health.

Consumer health risks

The pharmaceutical sector is a sensitive and important one, as the risk of counterfeit medicines implies for this sector not only possible economic damages but can also lead to significant health threats. This is because fake medicines are often not properly formulated and may contain dangerous ingredients; consumers are not very aware of the problem of counterfeiting and can be easily deceived into thinking that the products that they are purchasing are genuine.

This is confirmed by the existing evidence which stresses that fake medicines actually do create significant damage to consumer health (OECD/EUIPO, 2020[15]).

If all regions seem to be impacted by counterfeit medicines, it is important to note that Africa is particularly hit by this phenomenon, notably due to its distribution chain and the potential lack of pharmaceutical supply. Some studies highlight the scope and the negative effects of fake pharmaceuticals on patients' health in this region. According to a PricewaterhouseCoopers report, up to 70% of medicine in circulation across Africa may be fake. The Brazzaville Foundation also revealed that, every year, 120 000 children under the age of 5 die in Africa because of antimalarial medicine.[8]

The data challenge

From the data perspective, trade in counterfeit pharmaceuticals poses some additional challenges.

While customs data provide valuable information on the global trade of counterfeit pharmaceuticals, in the case of counterfeit pharmaceuticals they need to be complemented by other data sources. It is because a large share of this threat often falls outside the customs' scope. This is due to several factors, such as difficult identification of counterfeit medicines or new trends in trade in counterfeit medicines such as smuggling of raw ingredients and manufacturing of counterfeit medicines closer to the destination markets.

To address this issue, the following statistical analysis would benefit from other data sources to establish a more reliable and robust analysis on fake medicines.

An additional dataset used in this study is derived directly from the Swiss Pharmaceutical company Novartis. This database presents "incidents" that refer to fraudulent manufacture, mislabelling of drugs and fraudulent packaging. These incidents data have been established with the help of all kinds of enforcement agencies, such as police, health inspection service, customs, etc.

Both data sources are complementary and allow getting information on the infringement of Swiss pharmaceuticals brands from two different perspectives. For example, information derived from customs seizures on fake pharmaceuticals refer mostly to "common" pharmaceutical products (e.g. painkillers or erectile dysfunction treatment) while the broader data show that more medicine categories (such as cardiovascular, oncology treatment, etc.) are targeted by counterfeiters (OECD/EUIPO, 2020).

The trade in fake pharmaceuticals infringing Swiss IP rights holders

Illicit markets for counterfeit pharmaceuticals are attractive for counterfeiters, given their high profit margins, low risks of detection and prosecution, weak penalties and the ease with which consumers can be deceived into believing that the counterfeit products are genuine. According to recent estimates, in 2016, international trade in counterfeit pharmaceuticals reached USD 4.4 billion, threatening public health and safety, while enriching criminals and organised crime (OECD/EUIPO, 2020[15]). This does not include a very large volume of domestically produced and consumed illicit pharmaceuticals.

The impacts of counterfeit medicines are felt on many levels. The main area of impact is the damage to the health of patients and failure to treat their diseases properly. Another area is lost revenue for governments and economies.

A very important impact area of trade in fake medicines are losses of sales and damage to the reputations of legitimate producers. The OECD/EUIPO database (2019) on customs seizures indicates that US brands were largely the most affected by the trade in counterfeit pharmaceutical goods over the 2014-16 period, followed by European economies, including Austria, France, Germany, Switzerland and the UK (OECD/EUIPO, 2020[15])

According to the (OECD/EUIPO, 2020[15]) study, the value of global trade in counterfeit pharmaceuticals was up to USD 4.4 billion in 2016. This represents 0.84% of total worldwide imports in pharmaceutical products. China, India and some East Asian economies, including Indonesia, Pakistan, the Philippines and Viet Nam, appear to be the main producers of counterfeit pharmaceuticals traded worldwide (Table 3.9.).

Table 3.9. Main producing economies and transit points for counterfeit pharmaceutical products and medicines traded worldwide, 2014-16

Producing economy	Transit point
India	Hong Kong (China)
China (People's Republic of)	United Arab Emirates
Philippines	Egypt
Viet Nam	Cameroon
Indonesia	Turkey
Pakistan	Singapore

Note: Economies are listed in order of importance, indicating a greater likelihood that the economy in question is a producer or a transit point of counterfeit medicines in world trade.

The same report, by taking customs perspective and looking at the location of pharmaceutical companies that suffer from counterfeiting, concluded that Switzerland is the 7th country in the world(equally placed with France), after the US, Germany, the UK, Austria, China and India (see Figure 3.34). Globally, seized fakes that infringe Swiss IP represented 2.5% of the total seized value of fake pharmaceuticals in 2016.

Figure 3.34. Top economies of origin of pharmaceuticals right holders whose IP rights are infringed, 2011-16

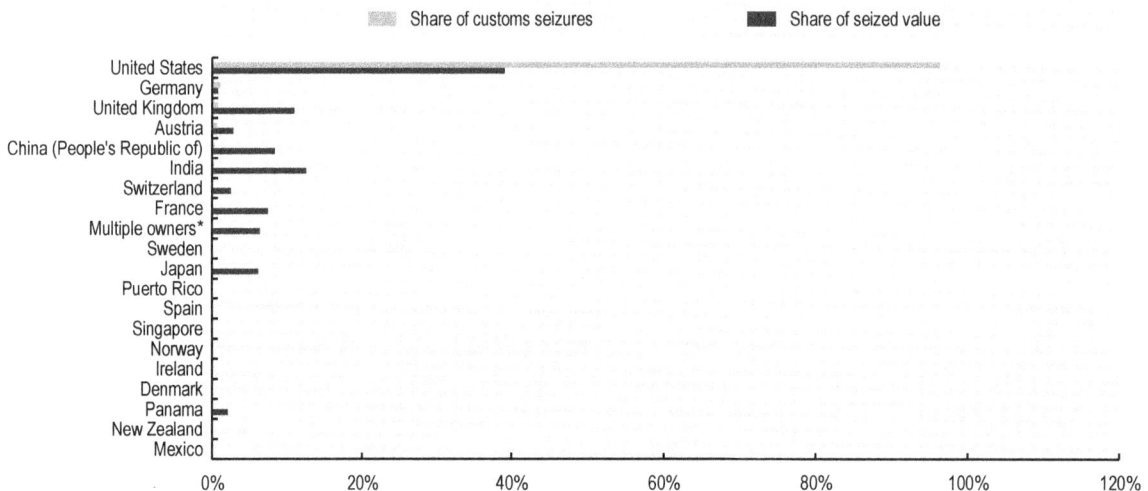

Source: OECD customs seizures database

Unfortunately, the data limitations for counterfeit pharmaceuticals do not allow a more robust, general analysis to be carried out. However, a more detailed dataset that permits a thorough analysis of one important right holder is possible. This is presented in the following section.

In addition, one can also present the available seizures customs data that infringed Swiss IP rights holders through some simple descriptive statistics analysis. Due to the limited datasets, this analysis was to a certain extent complemented with interviews with customs and industry experts. However, it still does not claim to provide a complete overview of trade in counterfeit pharmaceutical products that infringed Swiss IP. Rather, it provides general intuitive illustrations.

Counterfeit pharmaceutical products that infringed Swiss IP included antiepileptic drugs, psychotropic products, colpitis treatment, anaemia treatment and anxiolytic.

In terms of the economies of origin of fake medicines that infringe Swiss IP, during 2011-16, they mainly came from China (44% of customs seizures) followed by the UK, India and Egypt. China represented almost 100% of the seized value of fake Swiss pharmaceuticals during that period.

Over the 2017-19 period, most fake Swiss drugs originated mainly from China and India. In addition, Germany, Singapore and Hong Kong (China) were very important transit points. In addition, enforcement and industry experts highlight the point that a growing volume of infringement of Swiss IP in pharmaceuticals tends to occur close to the destination markets, for example in European Union countries. Criminals smuggle unbranded medicines and packaging (e.g. blisters and boxes) separately to minimise risks of seizures and reduce potential losses.

The COVID-19 crisis and trade in fake Swiss pharmaceuticals

The COVID-19 pandemic opens new opportunities for profits for criminals running illicit trade networks. Because of the pandemic, people, industry and governments require medicines and protective equipment and this demand often cannot be met in a timely fashion. Notably, the sharp market growth of illicit trade in pharmaceuticals refers not only to COVID-19-related medicines. Consequently, the COVID-19 pandemic creates additional opportunities for criminals that run networks for trade in illicit pharmaceuticals.

Due to lockdown, e-commerce is becoming one of the leading platforms for fake and substandard medicines that infringe the IP of Swiss pharmaceutical companies. Enforcement officials also highlight that those counterfeit medical products related to COVID-19 are often bought on line and shipped by air cargo in small parcels. Most of these products are produced in China and India, while Hong Kong (China) and Singapore remain the main transit hubs.

Concerning border enforcement, customs and police continue their efforts during the crisis. However, the pandemic poses additional challenges, particularly to customs, as with the high dynamism of changes in illicit networks, informative risk profiling becomes very difficult. This is reflected in available data; the rates of enforcement in 2020 dropped by 16% compared with 2019. This also calls for further dedicated awareness-raising efforts targeted at enforcement officials.

Illicit trade in fake medicines infringing Swiss IP rights keeps growing. Interviews with industry experts from Novartis point at the overall growth of 5% of average seizure value in 2020 compared with 2019. Considering the overall drop in enforcement, this suggests that trade in illicit medicines infringing Swiss IP rights has grown by 25% from 2019. Out of all these illicit medicines, 45% are counterfeits, while the remaining 55% came from either theft or diversion.

Infiltration of substandard or counterfeit products into the legitimate supply chain poses grave threats to public health and safety and the efforts to combat the spread of COVID-19. This collateral damage might grow in the future, as the pandemic's economic damages are likely to reduce the patients' purchasing power worldwide.

Focus on infringements of Novartis' IP

The additional dataset used in this section comes directly from Novartis, one of the main Swiss pharmaceutical companies. The data comprise cases on fraudulent manufacture, mislabelling of drugs and fraudulent packaging. This database originally refers to enforcement actions carried out by many kinds of enforcement agencies, such as police, health inspection services, customs, etc.

The data provided is organised into incidents. An incident is a discrete event triggered by the discovery of counterfeit, illegally diverted or stolen pharmaceuticals. An incident is a unique occurrence, with an assigned date, time, place and type of pharmaceutical product involved.

The OECD database on global customs seizures of counterfeit pharmaceuticals and the other enforcement database on incidents counterfeiting, theft and illegal diversion of pharmaceutical products worldwide are based on two completely different types of data collection. However, they can bring together a lot of information on the value and scope of the global market of illicit pharmaceuticals.

As can be seen in Figure 3.35, the number of incidents involving a Novartis product has grown steadily between 2016 and 2018 to 368. Data for 2019 show a decrease in the number of incidents, probably due to the fact that, in 2019, Novartis had separated from its ophthalmic branch, Alcon.

Figure 3.35. Total number of Novartis incidents, 2016-19

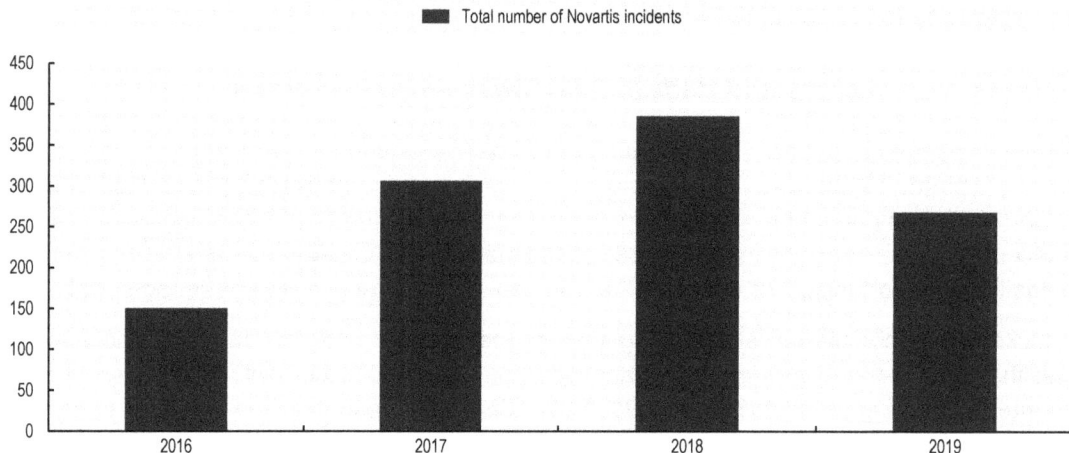

Note: The downward trend for 2019 may partly be explained by the fact that 2019 data excludes Alcon, as it is no longer one of Novartis' divisions.

In 2018, the share of incidents involving Novartis among worldwide incidents rose to almost 9%, a level similar to 2014 and 2018 but higher relative to 2015 and 2016 (around 5%). This means that, in 2018, almost 10% of incidents reported worldwide by pharmaceuticals companies were incidents involving the Swiss pharmaceuticals company.

Figure 3.36. Share of Novartis incidents among worldwide incidents

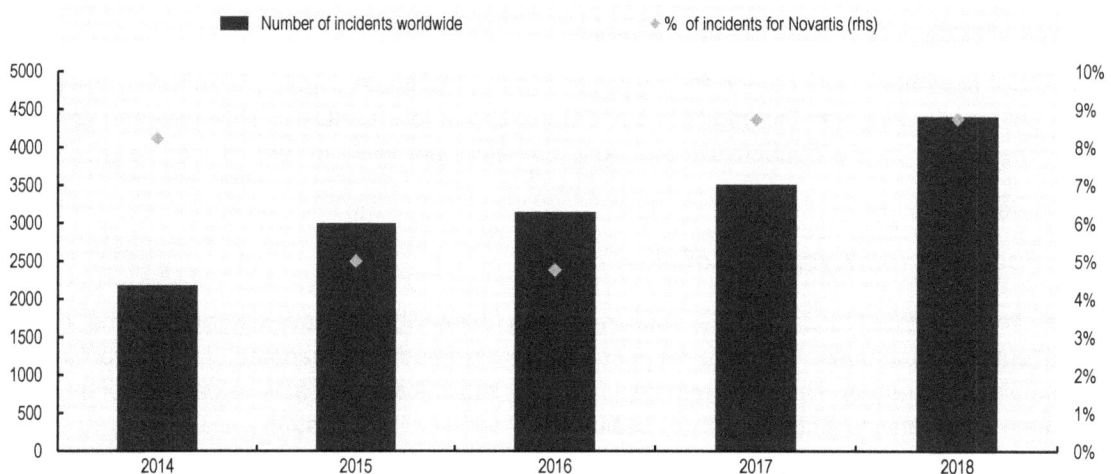

The infringement of Novartis IPR involved a large number of products since 64 Novartis pharmaceuticals have been counterfeited (see Table 3.10) in 2019. Overall, almost 120 Novartis pharmaceuticals have been subject to incidents in 2019, all types combined.

Table 3.10. Number of pharmaceuticals involved in Novartis incidents

Year	No. of pharmaceuticals involved in all incidents	No. of pharmaceuticals involved in counterfeiting incidents
2017	95	65
2018	148	58
2019	118	64

Note: In 2017, 95 Novartis pharmaceuticals have been involved in incidents, all types combined.

The data provided by the brand also specify the nature of the incidents, including product counterfeit, product diversion, product tampering and product theft. This means that these data cover a larger scope of incidents than data from customs that focus on counterfeit goods. Figure 3.37 displays the incidents involving Novartis products by incident types. This shows that product counterfeit and product diversion are the most frequent incidents while products tampering and theft are rarer. Indeed, in 2019 more than half of Novartis incidents involved counterfeiting and 31% involved product diversion.

Figure 3.37. Type of incidents involving Novartis products, 2016-19

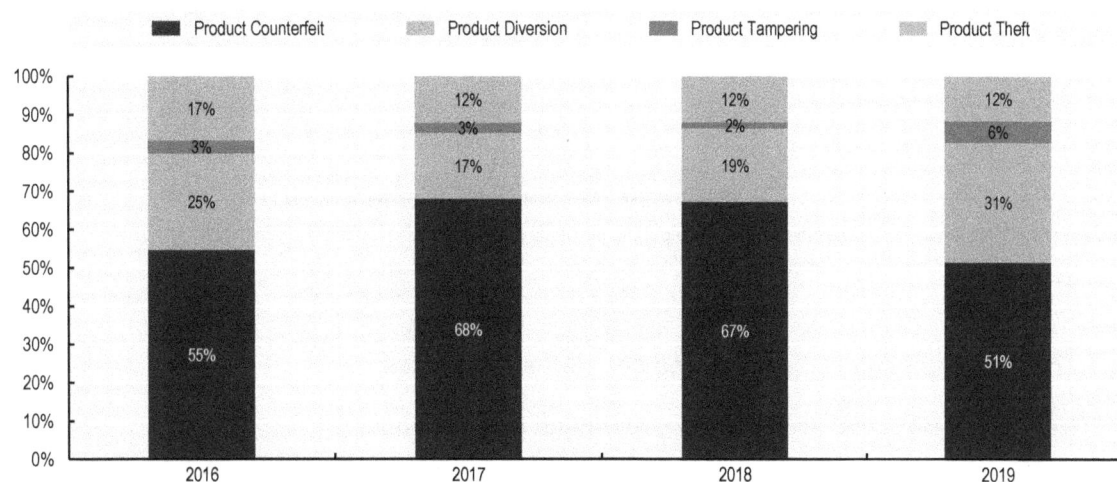

Note: In 2019, 51% of incidents involving Novartis pharmaceuticals were counterfeit product while the diversion represented 31%.

Of all counterfeit incidents, ophthalmology products were the therapeutic category the most targeted by counterfeiters (see Table 3.11.). In 2018, it represented 45% of Novartis counterfeit incidents, followed by cardiovascular treatment (10%), hormone growth medication (7%), anti-inflammatory medicines (3%) and oncology treatment (3%).

Table 3.11. Number of counterfeit incidents by therapeutic categories (top five), 2018

Therapeutic categories	Number of incidents	Share of total counterfeit incidents
Ophthalmology	117	45%
Cardiovascular	26	10%
Hormone growth	17	7%
Anti-inflammatory	8	3%
Oncology	7	3%

Note: Counterfeit Novartis ophthalmology products were the most targeted by counterfeiters in 2018, representing 45% of total counterfeit incidents involving Novartis products.

Table 3.12 displays the top ten countries reporting incidents. One can see that the US was the country linked to the highest number of incidents, reporting 88 incidents involving Novartis pharmaceuticals, followed by China (43 incidents reported) and India (16).

It is important to note that the frequency in reporting incidents is partly linked to rigorous government monitoring and active enforcement programmes. Consequently, countries reporting few (or no) incidents may probably be less involved in monitoring the pharmaceutical market.

Table 3.12. Top ten ranked reported incidents by country and incident type, 2018

Country	Incident type				
	Product counterfeit	Product diversion	Product tampering	Product theft	Total
United States	82	1	1	4	88
China (People's Republic of)	40		1	2	43
India	16	3			19
Colombia	12	2	1	2	17
Egypt	10	8			18
Germany	10	1	1	1	13
United Kingdom	6	2			8
Peru	5				5
Poland	5	1			6
Chile	3	1		2	6
Total	189	19	4	11	223

Note: With 88 reported incidents, the US was the 1st country reporting incidents that involved Novartis pharmaceuticals.

Box 3.5. Novartis' fight against falsified and counterfeit medicines

A brief overview of Novartis' actions to counter illicit fake products

The Swiss pharmaceuticals company which is involved in countering falsified and counterfeit medicines investigated 268 incidents of suspected falsified medicines in 2019. It led to 61 successful enforcement actions and the seizure of over 2 million falsified unit dosage medicines by law enforcement and health authorities and the dismantling of 11 illegal pharmaceutical manufacturing facilities. Among these dismantlements, a broad-scale assembly line in China was producing counterfeit cardiovascular treatments.

Novartis is also monitoring the most targeted Novartis products on online pharmacies, social media and commercial platforms which are an important distribution channel for fake pharmaceuticals. This monitoring led to 102 online investigations and the removal of 13 891 illegal listings in 2019.

The Swiss pharmaceuticals firms have also developed a tool to detect falsified medicines by performing non-invasive testing of a suspect sample to compare it to the library of genuine Novartis products.

References

OECD/EUIPO (2020), *Trade in Counterfeit Pharmaceutical Products*, Illicit Trade, OECD Publishing, Paris, https://dx.doi.org/10.1787/a7c7e054-en.   [15]

OECD/EUIPO (2019), *Trends in Trade in Counterfeit and Pirated Goods*, Illicit Trade, OECD Publishing, Paris, https://doi.org/10.1787/g2g9f533-en.   [11]

PSI (2019), *"Definition of counterfeiting, theft and illegal diversion", webpage, Pharmaceutical Security Institute*, Vienna, VA, https://www.psi-inc.org/pharma-crime.   [16]

Notes

[1] These industries correspond to the following categories classified by the Swiss Federal statistical office General Classification of Economic Activities (NOGA): 24, 25, 26 (except 2652), 27, 28, 29, 30, 325 and 33. These NOGA codes correspond to HS codes 72-90. See https://www.bfs.admin.ch/bfs/en/home/statistics/industry-services/nomenclatures/noga.html.

[2] Source: Eurostat.

[3] So far there are no structured statistics that could illustrate whether the growth of online counterfeiting has been proportional to the growth of e-commerce in general.

[4] Source: United Nations Comtrade database.

[5] BFS data for NACE R2 codes C10, C11, C2042 and C2053.

[6] Source: UN Comtrade database, 2014-16.

[7] For more information on the IP intensity of the pharmaceutical industry, see (OECD/EUIPO, 2020[15])

[8] For more information on the negative health effects of fake pharmaceuticals, see (OECD/EUIPO, 2020[15])

4. Concluding remarks

This chapter presents the main findings of the analysis and suggests some ways for further work.

Trade in fake Swiss goods: The impact on Switzerland

In assessing the global trade in goods that infringe Swiss intellectual property rights (IPRs), this report has shown the heavy impact of this illicit activity on Switzerland. The impact on the country's manufacturing industry is significant – equivalent to more than 0.7% of Swiss gross domestic product (GDP) and contributing to almost 11 000 lost jobs in 2018 alone, equivalent to 1.7% of all employees in Swiss manufacturing. It is not only industry affected but the impact on the Swiss government in lost revenues is also significant – amounting to almost USD 160 million in 2018.

The unique methodology deployed in this report has been used in three other country studies – Italy, Sweden and the United Kingdom (UK) – which could lead to a benchmarking exercise. In terms of jobs lost in the sector of domestic manufacturing, 27 000 jobs were lost in manufacturing in the UK (1.3% of total manufacturing employment) and 64 300 jobs in Italy (2.4%). The share of jobs lost in Switzerland (1.7%) is similar to the volume of jobs lost in other analysed countries. Foregone tax revenues amounted to 0.31% of UK GDP (GBP 897 million), 1.8% of Italian GDP (EUR 5.9 billion) and 0.12% of Swedish GDP (USD 680 million). The Swiss government revenue losses were lower than other countries due to its specific taxation profile. It is also important to note that losses experienced by Switzerland are underestimated due to a lack of data on the manufacturing industry at a detailed level.

While no sector is safe from counterfeiting, the watchmaking industry is by far the worst affected. Its sales losses amounted to CHF 1.99 billion (USD 2 billion) in 2018, or 45% of all lost sales across the Swiss manufacturing industry.

The impacts of counterfeiting and piracy can also be felt beyond Switzerland's borders – harming the consumers of Swiss goods worldwide. In unwittingly purchasing fake and low-quality products at inflated prices, consumers not only lose out financially, they also risk their health and safety. In 2019, this "consumer deception" due to the purchase of Swiss fake goods is estimated at almost CHF 2.06 billion (USD 2.07 billion).

The COVID-19 pandemic has deepened the crisis, exacerbating existing problems. The pandemic has had and will continue to have a significant impact on trade in counterfeit goods that infringe Swiss IPRs. The main factors that merit particular attention in this context are the very rapid boom of illicit offers on line, which results in the rapid growth of misuse of small parcels in trade in fakes that infringe the IPRs of Swiss right holders.

In addition, to meet the growing and unsatisfied demand for pharmaceuticals and personal protective equipment, criminals supply counterfeit products, machines to produce them and spare parts that often violate Swiss IPRs. Importantly, Swiss brands are often abused to add credibility to these substandard goods, even in cases when the legitimate right owner does offer products of a particular kind. Such practices clearly freeride on the high reputation of Swiss brands and can lead to brand erosion.

The magnitude of the issue and the scale of its impact should remain of high priority to both Swiss policymakers and the country's private sector. There are significant implications for the future, including those for activities that generate high value-added and those for innovation potential, both of which are sources of long-term economic growth.

Next steps

The magnitude of the issue and the scale of its impacts mean that tackling counterfeiting should remain of high priority to both Swiss policymakers and the private sector. There are significant implications for the future, including for activities that generate high value-added and those with innovation potential, both of which are sources of long-term economic growth.

These findings call for Switzerland to continue its strong involvement in international and multilateral initiatives to counter the risk of trade in counterfeit and pirated goods. This also includes the strengthening and co-ordination of information sharing across borders that becomes crucial to monitor the threat.

In addition, the rapid pace of changes during the COVID-19 pandemic underscores the need for an in-depth dialogue with private stakeholders, in particular in such areas as misuse of small parcels and the role of e-commerce. Such dialogue offers effective channels not only for information sharing but also provides good and flexible platforms for capacity building. In this context, the Stop Piracy initiative seems particularly relevant.

The methodology could also be successfully reapplied over time to detect trends in the scale and effects of counterfeiting and piracy in Switzerland. In addition, the methodology offers some flexibility in accommodating improvements in research, on substitution rates for example. This could lead to a more detailed analysis that would produce a more complete picture of trade in counterfeit and pirated goods, and its negative impact on rights holders, governments and consumers in Switzerland.

Annex A. Methodological notes

A.1. Primary and secondary markets

In order to distinguish fake products for sale by counterfeiters on the primary market from those intended for sale on the secondary market, the price difference between both types of counterfeits is calculated. For each seizure entered into the World Customs Organization (WCO) and European Commission Directorate-General for Taxation and Customs Union (DG TAXUD) databases, customs authorities report the infringed trademark, the declared value of goods, the quantity seized and the product's Harmonised System (HS) code. This allows the unit value of each seized "product type-brand" pair to be determined ("brand" includes the associated trademark or patent). These unit values can then serve as a proxy for the retail prices of fake goods.

For each type of product associated with a given trademark or patent, the prices of seized goods are used to estimate a confidence interval that contains the actual retail price of the corresponding genuine item. Counterfeit items whose unit price, calculated as described above, is higher than or included in this interval are then classified as intended for sale on the primary market. Those whose price is below this interval are classified as targeting the secondary market.

Formally, let s_c and $\bar{s}_c$ denote, respectively, the import value and quantity of any custom seizure of counterfeit products, with $c \in \{1, \dots, N\}$ the range of customs seizures and N their total number. $p_c = s_c/\bar{s}_c$ then refers to the unit value of each custom seizure and can serve as a proxy for their unit price. Let $p_{bp} = \left(\sum_{c\in\{bp\}} p_c\right)/N_{bp}$ define the (unweighted) price average of any type of product p associated with the brand or patent b, with N_{bp} the total number of custom seizures reported for this "product category-brand" combination. The standard deviation of this price is denoted σ_{bp}.

X_c is defined as a dichotomous (binary) variable that takes the value of 0 if the fake goods included in the seized shipment were intended to be sold on the primary market, or 1 if they were intended to be sold on the secondary market. In accordance with the arguments mentioned in the main text, X_c is assumed to be defined as follows:

$$X_c = \begin{cases} = 0 \text{ if } p_c \in \left[p_{bp} - \dfrac{1.96 \times \sigma_{bp}}{\sqrt{N_{bp}}} ; \max_{c\in\{bp\}} p_c\right] \\ = 1 \text{ if } p_c \in \left[\min_{c\in\{bp\}} p_c ; p_{bp} - \dfrac{1.96 \times \sigma_{bp}}{\sqrt{N_{bp}}}\right[\end{cases} ; \quad \forall c\{bp\}$$

It follows that the share of products sold on the primary market can be calculated by product category, τ_p^1, and/or for the entire mass of fake imports, and is given by:

$$\tau_p^1 = \left(\sum_b \sum_c X_c s_c\right) / \left(\sum_b \sum_c s_c\right), \quad \forall c\in\{bp\}$$

For example, Figure A A.1 shows the price distribution of fake shoes of brand X that were seized by global customs between 2014 and 2016. Using the methodology outlined above, this indicates that most fake X shoes with prices lower than USD 121 were destined for the secondary market, while those with values higher than USD 121 (observations in the middle and on the right-hand side of the distribution) were targeted at the primary market.

Figure A A.1. Price distribution of fake shoes of brand X seized by global customs, 2014-16

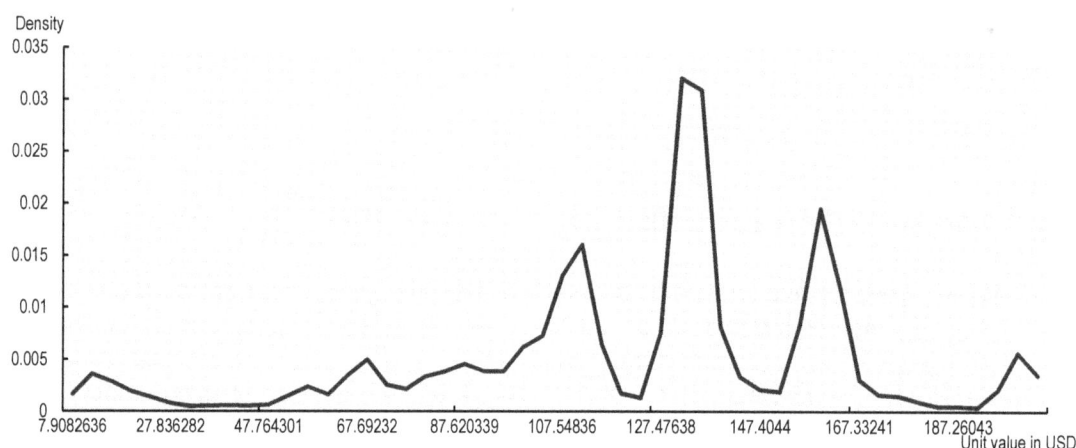

A.2. Constructing the General Trade-Related Index of Counterfeiting for products (GTRIC-p)

GTRIC-p is constructed through four steps:

1. For each reporting economy, the seizure percentages for sensitive goods are calculated.

2. For each product category, aggregate seizure percentages are calculated, taking the reporting economies' share of total sensitive imports as weights.

3. From these, a counterfeit source factor is established for each industry, based on the industries' weight in terms of total trade.

4. Based on these factors, the GTRIC-p is calculated.

Step 1: Measuring reporter-specific product seizure intensities

$\tilde{v}_i^k$ and $\tilde{m}_i^k$ are, respectively, the seizure and import values of product type k (as registered according to the HS on the two-digit level) in economy i from *any* provenance economy in a given year. Economy i's relative seizure intensity (seizure percentages) of good k, denoted below as γ_i^k is then defined as:

$$\gamma_i^k = \frac{\tilde{v}_i^k}{\sum_{k=1}^{\bar{K}} \tilde{v}_i^k}, \text{ such that } \sum_{k=1}^{\bar{K}} \gamma_i^k = 1 \ \forall \ i \ \in \{1, \dots, \bar{N}\}$$

$k = \{1, \dots, \bar{K}\}$ is the range of sensitive goods (the total number of goods is given by K) and $i = \{1, \dots, \bar{N}\}$ is the range of reporting economies (the total number of economies is given by N).

Step 2: Measuring general product seizure intensities

The general seizure intensity for product k, denoted $\mathbf{\Gamma}^k$, is then determined by averaging seizure intensities, γ_i^k, weighted by the reporting economies' share of total sensitive imports in a given product category, k. Hence:

$$\Gamma^k = \sum_{i=1}^{\bar{N}} \omega_i \gamma_i^k \ , \ \forall \ k \ \in \{1, \dots, \bar{K}\}$$

The weight of reporting economy i is given by:

$$\omega_i = \frac{\widetilde{m}_i^k}{\sum_{i=1}^{\widetilde{N}} \widetilde{m}_i^k}$$

where $\widetilde{m}_i$ is i's total registered import value of sensitive goods ($\sum_{i=1}^{\widetilde{n}} \omega_i = 1$)

Step 3: Measuring product-specific counterfeiting factors

$\widetilde{M}_i^k = \sum_{i=1}^N \widetilde{m}_i^k$ is defined as the total registered imports of sensitive good k for *all* economies and $\widetilde{M} = \sum_{k=1}^{\widetilde{K}} \widetilde{M}^k$ is defined as the total registered world imports of *all* sensitive goods.

The world import share of good k, denoted s^k, is therefore given by:

$$s^k = \frac{\widetilde{M}^k}{\widetilde{M}}, \text{ such that } \sum_{k=1}^{\widetilde{K}} s^k = 1$$

The general counterfeiting factor of product category k, denoted CP^k, is then determined as the following:

$$CP^k = \frac{\Gamma^k}{s^k}$$

The counterfeiting factor reflects the sensitivity of product infringements occurring in a particular product category, relative to its share in international trade. These are based on the seizure percentages calculated for each reporting economy and constitute the foundation of the formation of GTRIC-p.

Step 4: Establishing GTRIC-p

GTRIC-p is constructed from a transformation of the general counterfeiting factor and measures the relative likelihood that different product categories will be subject to counterfeiting and piracy in international trade. The transformation of the counterfeiting factor is based on two main assumptions:

- Assumption (A1): The counterfeiting factor of a particular product category is positively correlated with the actual intensity of international trade in counterfeit and pirated goods covered by that chapter. The counterfeiting factors must thus reflect the real intensity of actual counterfeit trade in the given product categories.

- Assumption (A2): This acknowledges that the assumption A1 may not be entirely correct. For instance, the fact that infringing goods are detected more frequently in certain categories could imply that differences in counterfeiting factors across products merely reflect that some goods are easier to detect than others or that some goods, for one reason or another, have been specially targeted for inspection. The counterfeiting factors of product categories with lower counterfeiting factors could, therefore, underestimate actual counterfeiting and piracy intensities in these cases.

In accordance with assumption A1 (positive correlation between counterfeiting factors and actual infringement activities) and assumption A2 (lower counterfeiting factors may underestimate actual activities), GTRIC-p is established by applying a positive monotonic transformation of the counterfeiting factor index using natural logarithms. This standard technique of linearisation of a non-linear relationship (in the case of this study between counterfeiting factors and actual infringement activities) allows the index to be flattened and gives a higher relative weight to lower counterfeiting factors (Verbeek, 2000[17]).

In order to address the possibility of outliers at both ends of the counterfeiting factor index (i.e. some categories may be measured as particularly susceptible to infringement even though they are not, whereas others may be measured as insusceptible although they are), it is assumed that GTRIC-p follows a left-truncated normal distribution, with GTRIC-p only taking values of zero or above.

The transformed counterfeiting factor is defined as:

$$cp^k = \ln(CP^k + 1)$$

Assuming that the transformed counterfeiting factor can be described by a left-truncated normal distribution with $cp^k \geq 0$, then, following Hald (1952[18]), the density function of GTRIC-p is given by:

$$f_{LTN}(cp^k) = \begin{cases} 0 & if \ cp^k \leq 0 \\ \dfrac{f(cp^k)}{\int_0^\infty f(cp^k)dcp^k} & if \ cp^k \geq 0 \end{cases}$$

where $f(cp^k)$ is the non-truncated normal distribution for cp^k specified as:

$$f(cp^k) = \frac{1}{\sqrt{2\pi\sigma_{cp}^2}} exp\left(-\frac{1}{2}\left(\frac{(cp^k) - \mu_{cp}}{\sigma_{cp}}\right)^2\right)$$

The mean and variance of the normal distribution, here denoted μ_{cp} and σ_{cp}^2, are estimated over the transformed counterfeiting factor index, cp^k, and given by $\hat{\mu}_{cp}^2$ and σ_{cp}^2. This enables the calculation of the counterfeit import propensity index (GTRIC-p) across HS codes, corresponding to the cumulative distribution function of cp^k.

A.3. Constructing the general trade-related index of counterfeiting economies (GTRIC-e)

GTRIC-e is also constructed through four steps:

1. For each reporting economy, the seizure percentages for provenance economies are calculated.
2. For each provenance economy, aggregate seizure percentages are calculated, taking the reporting economies' share of total sensitive imports as weights.
3. From these, each economy's counterfeit source factor is established, based on the provenance economies' weight in terms of total trade.
4. Based on these factors, the GTRIC-e is calculated.

Step 1: Measuring reporter-specific seizure intensities from each provenance economy

$\tilde{v}_i^j$ is economy i's registered seizures of all types of infringing goods (i.e. all *k*) originating from economy *j* in a given year in terms of their value. γ_i^j is economy i's relative seizure intensity (seizure percentage) of all infringing items that originate from economy *j*, in a given year:

$$\gamma_i^j = \frac{\tilde{v}_i^j}{\Sigma_{j=1}^{\bar{J}}\tilde{v}_i^j} \text{ such that } \Sigma_{j=1}^{\bar{J}}\gamma_i^j = 1 \ \forall \ i \ \in \{1, ..., \bar{N}\}$$

Where $j = \{1, ..., \bar{J}\}$ is the range of identified provenance economies (the total number of exporters is given by J) and $i = \{1, ..., \bar{N}\}$ is the range of reporting economies (the total number of economies is given by N).

Step 2: Measuring general seizure intensities of each provenance economy

The general seizure intensity for economy j, denoted Γ^j, is then determined by averaging seizure intensities, γ_i^j, weighted by the reporting economy's share of total imports from known counterfeit and pirate origins.[1] Hence:

$$\Gamma^j = \textstyle\sum_{i=1}^{\bar{N}} \omega_i \gamma_i^j , \ \forall j \ \in \{1, ..., \bar{J}\}$$

The weight of reporting economy i is given by:

$$\omega_i = \frac{\tilde{m}_i^j}{\sum_{i=1}^{\bar{N}} \tilde{m}_i^j}, \text{ such that } \textstyle\sum_{i=1}^{\bar{N}} \omega_i = 1$$

Step 3: Measuring partner-specific counterfeiting factors

$\bar{M}_i^j = \sum_{i=1}^{N} \tilde{m}_i^j$ is defined as the total registered world imports of all sensitive products from j,[2] and $\bar{M} = \sum_{j=1}^{\bar{J}} \bar{M}^j$ is the total world import of sensitive goods from all provenance economies.

The share of imports from provenance economy j in total world imports of sensitive goods, denoted s^j, is then given by:

$$s^j = \frac{\bar{M}^j}{\bar{M}}, \text{ such that } \textstyle\sum_{j=1}^{\bar{J}} s^j = 1$$

From this, the economy-specific counterfeiting factor is established by dividing the general seizure intensity for economy j by the share of total imports of sensitive goods from j.

$$CE^j = \frac{\Gamma^j}{s^j}$$

Step 4: Establishing GTRIC-e

Gauging the magnitude of counterfeiting and piracy from a provenance economy perspective can be done in a similar fashion as for sensitive goods. Hence, a General Trade-Related Index of Counterfeiting for economies (GTRIC-e) is established along similar lines and assumptions:

- Assumption (A3): The intensity by which any counterfeit or pirated article from a particular economy is detected and seized by customs is positively correlated with the actual amount of counterfeit and pirate articles imported from that location.

- Assumption (A4): This acknowledges that assumption A3 may not be entirely correct. For instance, a high seizure intensity of counterfeit or pirated articles from a particular provenance economy could be an indication that the provenance economy is part of a customs profiling scheme or that it is specially targeted for investigation by customs. The importance that provenance economies with low seizure intensities play regarding actual counterfeiting and piracy activity could, therefore, be under-represented by the index and lead to an underestimation of the scale of counterfeiting and piracy.

As with the product-specific index, GTRIC-e is established by applying a positive monotonic transformation of the counterfeiting factor index for provenance economies using natural logarithms. This follows from assumption A3 (positive correlation between seizure intensities and actual infringement activities) and assumption A4 (lower intensities tend to underestimate actual activities). Considering the possibilities of outliers at both ends of the GTRIC e-distribution (i.e. some economies may be wrongly measured as being particularly susceptible sources of counterfeit and pirated imports, and vice versa), GTRIC-e is approximated by a left-truncated normal distribution as it does not take values below zero.

The transformed general counterfeiting factor across provenance economies on which GTRIC-e is based is therefore given by applying logarithms onto economy-specific general counterfeit factors (see, for example, Verbeek (2000[17])):

$$ce^j = ln(CE^j + 1)$$

In addition, following GTRIC-p, it is assumed that GTRIC-e follows a truncated normal distribution with $ce^j \geq 0$ for all j. Following Hald (1952[18]), the density function of the left-truncated normal distribution for ce^j is given by:

$$g_{LTN}(ce^j) = \begin{cases} 0 & if \ ce^j \leq 0 \\ \dfrac{g(ce^j)}{\int_0^\infty g(ce^j)dce} & if \ ce^j \geq 0 \end{cases}$$

where $g(ce^j)$ is the non-truncated normal distribution for ce^j specified as:

$$g(ce^j) = \frac{1}{\sqrt{2\pi\sigma_{ce}^2}} exp\left(-\frac{1}{2}\left(\frac{ce^j - \mu_{ce}}{\sigma_{ce}}\right)^2\right)$$

The mean and variance of the normal distribution, here denoted μ_{ce} and σ_{ce}^2, are estimated over the transformed counterfeiting factor index, ce^j, and given by $\hat{\mu}_{ce}$ and $\hat{\sigma}_{ce}^2$. This enables the calculation of the counterfeit import propensity index (GTRIC-e) across provenance economies, corresponding to the cumulative distribution function of ce^j.

A.4. Constructing the General Trade-Related Index of Counterfeiting (GTRIC)

In the OECD (2008[19]) and OECD/EUIPO (2016[7]) studies, propensities to import infringing goods from different trading partners were developed using seizure data as a basis. The use of data is maximised by applying a generalised approach in which the propensities for products to be counterfeit and for economies to be sources of counterfeit goods were analysed separately. This increased the data coverage of both products and provenance economies significantly, which increases the robustness of the overall estimation results. Unfortunately, it also reduced the detail of the analysis, meaning that counterfeit trade patterns specific to individual reporting economies, for both product types and trading partners, were not simultaneously accounted for; this introduced bias into the results. On balance, however, given the large scope of the analysis, the advantages of increasing data coverage can be viewed as outweighing the biases.

This approach combines the two indices: GTRIC-p and GTRIC-e. In this regard, it is important to emphasise that the index resulting from this combination does not account for differences in infringement intensities across different types of goods that may exist between economies. For instance, imports of certain counterfeit and pirated goods could be particularly large from some trading partners and small from others. An index taking such "infringement specialisation", or concentration, into account is desirable and possible to construct; but it would require detailed seizure data. The combined index, denoted GTRIC, is, therefore, a generalised index that approximates the relative likelihoods that particular product types, imported from specific trading partners, are counterfeit and/or pirated.

Establishing likelihoods for product and provenance economy

In this step, for each trade flow from a given provenance economy and for a given product category the likelihoods of containing counterfeit and pirated products will be established.

The general propensity for an economy to export infringed items of HS category k is denoted P^k, and given by GTRIC-p, so that:

$$P^k = F_{LTN}(cp^k)$$

where $F_{LTN}(cp^k)$ is the cumulative probability function of $f_{LTN}(cp^k)$.

Furthermore, the general likelihood of importing any type of infringing goods from economy j is denoted as P^j, and given by GTRIC-e, so that:

$$P^j = G_{LTN}(ce^j)$$

where $G_{LTN}(ce^j)$ is the cumulative probability function of $f_{LTN}(ce^j)$.

The general probability of importing counterfeit or pirated items of type k originating from economy j is then denoted P^{jk} and approximated by:

$$P^{jk} = P^k P^j$$

Therefore, $P^{jk} \in [\varepsilon_p \varepsilon_e; 1)$, $\forall j, k$, with $\varepsilon_p \varepsilon_e$ denoting the minimum average counterfeit export rate for each sensitive product category and each provenance economy,[3] it is assumed that $\varepsilon_p = \varepsilon_e = 0.05$.

A.5. Calculating the absolute value

α is the fixed point, i.e. the maximum average counterfeit import rate of a given type of infringing good, k, originating from a given trading partner, j.

α can be applied to propensities for importing infringing goods of type j from trading partner k (αP^{jk}). As a result, a matrix of counterfeit import propensities **C** is obtained.

$$C = \begin{pmatrix} \alpha P^{11} & \alpha P^{21} & & \alpha P^{1K} \\ \alpha P^{12} & \ddots & & \\ \vdots & & \alpha P^{jk} & \vdots \\ & & & \ddots \\ \alpha P^{J1} & & & \alpha P^{JK} \end{pmatrix} \text{ with dimension } J \times K$$

The matrix of world imports is denoted by **M**. Applying **C** on **M** yields the absolute volume of trade in counterfeit and pirated goods.

In particular, the import matrix **M** is given by:

$$M = \begin{pmatrix} M_1 \\ \vdots \\ M_i \\ \vdots \\ M_n \end{pmatrix} \text{ with dimension } n \times J \times K$$

Each element is defined by economy i's unique import matrix of good k from trading partner j.

$$M_i = \begin{pmatrix} m_{i1}^1 & m_{i1}^2 & & & m_{i1}^K \\ m_{i2}^1 & \ddots & & & \\ \vdots & & m_{ij}^k & & \vdots \\ & & & \ddots & \\ m_{ij}^1 & & & & m^{JK} \end{pmatrix} \text{ with dimension } J \times K$$

Hence, the element m_{ij}^k denotes i's imports of product category k from trading partner j, where $i = \{1, \ldots, n\}$, $j = \{1, \ldots, J\}$, and $k = \{1, \ldots, K\}$.

Denoted by Ψ, the product-by-economy percentage of counterfeit and pirated imports can be determined as the following:

$$\Psi = C'M \div M$$

Total trade in counterfeit and pirated goods, denoted by the scalar **TC**, is then given by:

$$TC = i_1'\Psi i_2$$

where i_1 is a vector of one with dimension $nJ \times 1$, and i_2 is a vector of one with dimension $K \times 1$. Then, by denoting total world trade by the scalar $TM = i_1'Mi_2$, the value of counterfeiting and piracy in world trade, s_{TC}, is determined by:

$$s_{TC} = \frac{TC}{TM}$$

A.6. Consumer detriment

Individual consumer detriment is the price premium unjustly paid by the consumer in the belief they are buying a genuine product. As consumers who choose to purchase counterfeit products on secondary markets deliberately accept a cost-quality trade-off, consumer detriment only occurs in primary markets. For each product category, the individual consumer detriment is estimated by calculating the difference between the average price paid in the primary market (by deceived consumers) and that paid in the secondary market (by consumers who knowingly buy fake goods). This individual consumer detriment is then multiplied by the total volume of transactions in the primary market in a given product category. Finally, for all product categories, the detriments are added together to give a general estimate of overall consumer detriment.

More formally, the principle behind the measure of consumer detriment is as follows. First, for any type of product p related to brand b, the average price paid on the primary market, p_{bp}^1, and the average price paid on the secondary market, p_{bp}^2, are calculated. Since the gap between these prices represents the "value of consumers' deception", it can be used as a proxy for the consumer detriment of purchasing a given branded product bp on the primary market: $d_{bp} = p_{bp}^1 - p_{bp}^2$. Finally, these detriments can be aggregated by product category or, at the national level, by multiplying them by the estimated volume of sales on primary markets, Q_{bp}^1, as follows: $D = \sum_b \sum_p (d_{bp} Q_{bp}^1)$.

References

Hald, A. (1952), *Statistical Theory with Engineering Applications*, John Wiley and Sons, New York.   [18]

OECD (2008), *The Economic Impact of Counterfeiting and Piracy*, OECD Publishing, Paris, http://dx.doi.org/10.1787/9789264045521-en.   [19]

OECD/EUIPO (2016), *Trade in Counterfeit and Pirated Goods: Mapping the Economic Impact*, OECD Publishing, Paris, http://dx.doi.org/10.1787/9789264252653-en.   [7]

Verbeek, M. (2000), *A Guide to Modern Econometrics*, Wiley.   [17]

Notes

[1] This is different to the economy's share of total imports of sensitive goods used to calculate GTRIC-p.

[2] This is different to the total imports of sensitive goods as used in calculation of GTRIC-p.

[3] In the OECD (2008[19]) methodology, these factors were applied to all provenance economies and all HS modules in order to account for counterfeit and pirated exports of products and/or from provenance economies that were not identified. This assumption is relaxed in this study, given the overall good data quality.

Annex B. Tables and figures

Table B.1. ISO codes for countries and territories

ISO3 code	Economy
AND	Andorra
ARE	United Arab Emirates
AFG	Afghanistan
ATG	Antigua and Barbuda
AIA	Anguilla
ALB	Albania
ARM	Armenia
ANT	Netherlands Antilles
AGO	Angola
ATA	Antarctica
ARG	Argentina
ASM	American Samoa
AUT	Austria
AUS	Australia
ABW	Aruba
ALA	Åland
AZE	Azerbaijan
BIH	Bosnia and Herzegovina
BRB	Barbados
BGD	Bangladesh
BEL	Belgium
BFA	Burkina Faso
BGR	Bulgaria
BHR	Bahrain
BDI	Burundi
BEN	Benin
BLM	Saint-Barthélemy
BMU	Bermuda
BRN	Brunei Darussalam
BOL	Bolivia
BES	Bonaire
BRA	Brazil
BHS	Bahamas
BTN	Bhutan
BVT	Bouvet Island
BWA	Botswana
BLR	Belarus
BLZ	Belize
CAN	Canada
CCK	Cocos (Keeling) Islands
COD	Democratic Republic of the Congo
CAF	Central African Republic
COG	Congo
CHE	Switzerland
CIV	Côte d'Ivoire

COK	Cook Islands
CHL	Chile
CMR	Cameroon
CHN	China (People's Republic of)
COL	Colombia
CRI	Costa Rica
CUB	Cuba
CPV	Cabo Verde
CUW	Curaçao
CXR	Christmas Island
CYP	Cyprus*
CZE	Czech Republic
DEU	Germany
DJI	Djibouti
DNK	Denmark
DMA	Dominica
DOM	Dominican Republic
DZA	Algeria
ECU	Ecuador
EST	Estonia
EGY	Egypt
ESH	Western Sahara
ERI	Eritrea
ESP	Spain
ETH	Ethiopia
FIN	Finland
FJI	Fiji
FLK	Falkland Islands (Malvinas)
FSM	Micronesia
FRO	Faroe Islands
FRA	France
GAB	Gabon
GBR	United Kingdom
GRD	Grenada
GEO	Georgia
GUF	French Guiana
GGY	Guernsey
GHA	Ghana
GIB	Gibraltar
GRL	Greenland
GMB	Gambia
GIN	Guinea
GLP	Guadeloupe
GNQ	Equatorial Guinea
GRC	Greece
SGS	South Georgia and the South Sandwich Islands
GTM	Guatemala
GUM	Guam
GNB	Guinea-Bissau
GUY	Guyana
HKG	Hong Kong (China)
HMD	Heard Island and McDonald Islands
HND	Honduras
HRV	Croatia
HTI	Haiti
HUN	Hungary
IDN	Indonesia

IRL	Ireland
ISR	Israel
IMN	Isle of Man
IND	India
IOT	British Indian Ocean Territory
IRQ	Iraq
IRN	Iran
ISL	Iceland
ITA	Italy
JEY	Jersey
JAM	Jamaica
JOR	Jordan
JPN	Japan
KEN	Kenya
KGZ	Kyrgyzstan
KHM	Cambodia
KIR	Kiribati
COM	Comoros
KNA	Saint Kitts and Nevis
PRK	Democratic People's Republic of Korea
KOR	Korea
KWT	Kuwait
CYM	Cayman Islands
KAZ	Kazakhstan
LAO	Lao People's Democratic Republic
LBN	Lebanon
LCA	Saint Lucia
LIE	Liechtenstein
LKA	Sri Lanka
LBR	Liberia
LSO	Lesotho
LTU	Lithuania
LUX	Luxembourg
LVA	Latvia
LBY	Libya
MAR	Morocco
MCO	Monaco
MDA	Moldova
MNE	Montenegro
MAF	Saint Martin
MDG	Madagascar
MHL	Marshall Islands
MKD	Former Yugoslav Republic of Macedonia
MLI	Mali
MMR	Myanmar
MNG	Mongolia
MAC	Macau (China)
MNP	Northern Mariana Islands
MTQ	Martinique
MRT	Mauritania
MSR	Montserrat
MLT	Malta
MUS	Mauritius
MDV	Maldives
MWI	Malawi
MEX	Mexico
MYS	Malaysia

MOZ	Mozambique
NAM	Namibia
NCL	New Caledonia
NER	Niger
NFK	Norfolk Island
NGA	Nigeria
NIC	Nicaragua
NLD	Netherlands
NOR	Norway
NPL	Nepal
NRU	Nauru
NIU	Niue
NZL	New Zealand
OMN	Oman
PAN	Panama
PER	Peru
PYF	French Polynesia
PNG	Papua New Guinea
PHL	Philippines
PAK	Pakistan
POL	Poland
SPM	Saint Pierre and Miquelon
PCN	Pitcairn
PRI	Puerto Rico
PSE	Palestinian Authority*
PRT	Portugal
PLW	Palau
PRY	Paraguay
QAT	Qatar
REU	Réunion
ROU	Romania
SRB	Serbia
RUS	Russia
RWA	Rwanda
SAU	Saudi Arabia
SLB	Solomon Islands
SYC	Seychelles
SDN	Sudan
SWE	Sweden
SGP	Singapore
SHN	Saint Helena
SVN	Slovenia
SJM	Svalbard and Jan Mayen
SVK	Slovak Republic
SLE	Sierra Leone
SMR	San Marino
SEN	Senegal
SOM	Somalia
SUR	Suriname
SSD	South Sudan
STP	Sao Tome and Principe
SLV	El Salvador
SXM	Sint Maarten
SYR	Syrian Arab Republic
SWZ	Swaziland
TCA	Turks and Caicos Islands
TCD	Chad

ATF	French Southern and Antarctic Lands
TGO	Togo
THA	Thailand
TJK	Tajikistan
TKL	Tokelau
TLS	Timor-Leste
TKM	Turkmenistan
TUN	Tunisia
TON	Tonga
TUR	Turkey
TTO	Trinidad and Tobago
TUV	Tuvalu
TWN	Chinese Taipei*
TZA	Tanzania
UKR	Ukraine
UGA	Uganda
UMI	United States Minor Outlying Islands
USA	United States
URY	Uruguay
UZB	Uzbekistan
VAT	Holy See
VCT	Saint Vincent and the Grenadines
VEN	Venezuela
VGB	British Virgin Islands
VIR	United States Virgin Islands
VNM	Viet Nam
VUT	Vanuatu
WLF	Wallis and Futuna
WSM	Samoa
XKO	Kosovo
YEM	Yemen
MYT	Mayotte
ZAF	South Africa
ZMB	Zambia
ZWE	Zimbabwe

Note: * The information in this document with reference to "Cyprus" relates to the southern part of the Island. There is no single authority representing both Turkish and Greek Cypriot people on the Island. Turkey recognises the Turkish Republic of Northern Cyprus (TRNC). Until a lasting and equitable solution is found within the context of the UN, Turkey shall preserve its position concerning the "Cyprus issue".

The Republic of Cyprus is recognised by all members of the UN with the exception of Turkey. The information in this document relates to the area under the effective control of the Government of the Republic of Cyprus.

Table B.2. Likelihood that product categories will be targeted by infringements of Swiss IPR

GTRIC-p for goods infringing Swiss IPR, 2014-16

	2014	2015	2016
Aircraft (88)	0.000	0.000	0.000
Arms and ammunition (93)	0.000	0.000	0.000
Articles of leather; handbags (42)	0.856	0.756	0.838
Articles of stone, plaster and cement (68)	0.000	0.000	0.000
Beverages (22)	0.000	0.000	0.000
Carpets and rugs (57)	0.000	0.000	0.000
Ceramic products (69)	0.023	0.009	0.019
Clothing and accessories, not knitted or crocheted (62/65)	0.100	0.048	0.087
Clothing, knitted or crocheted (61)	0.999	0.996	0.999
Copper; nickel; aluminium; lead; zinc; tin; and articles thereof (74-81)	0.000	0.000	0.000
Cork; straw and articles thereof (45/46)	0.000	0.000	0.000
Electrical machinery and electronics (85)	0.248	0.147	0.225
Fertilisers (31)	0.000	0.000	0.000
Finishing of textiles (58)	0.014	0.005	0.012
Foodstuffs (02-21)	0.181	0.100	0.162
Footwear (64)	0.422	0.286	0.392
Furniture (94)	0.185	0.102	0.165
Fur skins and artificial fur (43)	0.000	0.000	0.000
Glass and glassware (70)	0.152	0.080	0.135
Iron and steel; and articles thereof (72/73)	0.018	0.006	0.015
Jewellery (71)	0.178	0.097	0.158
Knitted or crocheted fabrics (60)	0.305	0.189	0.279
Label	0.181	0.100	0.162
Machinery and mechanical appliances (84)	0.168	0.091	0.149
Man-made filaments and staple fibres (54/55)	0.000	0.000	0.000
Mineral fuels (27)	0.000	0.000	0.000
Miscellaneous articles of base metal (83)	0.000	0.000	0.000
Miscellaneous chemical products (38)	0.193	0.107	0.173
Miscellaneous manufactured articles (66/67/96)	0.560	0.415	0.530
Musical instruments (92)	0.000	0.000	0.000
Optical; photographic; medical apparatus (90)	0.180	0.099	0.161
Ores, slag and ash (26)	0.000	0.000	0.000
Organic and inorganic chemicals (28/29)	0.000	0.000	0.000
Other made up textile articles (63)	0.142	0.074	0.126
Other textiles n.e.c.* (59)	0.014	0.005	0.012
Perfumery and cosmetics (33)	0.349	0.224	0.321
Pharmaceutical products (30)	0.115	0.058	0.101
Plastic and articles thereof (39)	0.142	0.074	0.125
Printed articles (49)	0.038	0.015	0.032
Pulp and paper (47/48)	0.070	0.032	0.060
Railway (86)	0.000	0.000	0.000
Raw hides, skins and leather (41)	0.000	0.000	0.000
Residues from the food industries (23)	0.000	0.000	0.000
Rubber and article thereof (40)	0.000	0.000	0.000
Salt; sulphur; earths and stone; lime and cement (25)	0.000	0.000	0.000
Ships (89)	0.000	0.000	0.000
Silk; wool; and other vegetable textile fibres (50-53)	0.000	0.000	0.000
Soap; albuminoidal substances; glues; explosives (34-37)	0.000	0.000	0.000
Tanning or dyeing extracts (32)	0.028	0.011	0.023
Tobacco (24)	1.000	1.000	1.000
Tools and cutlery of base metal (82)	0.087	0.041	0.075
Toys and games (95)	0.679	0.539	0.652

Vehicles (87)	0.025	0.009	0.021
Wadding; cordage; ropes and articles thereof (56)	0.000	0.000	0.000
Watches (91)	1.000	0.999	1.000
Wood and articles thereof (44)	0.000	0.000	0.000
Works of art, collectors' pieces and antiques (97)	0.000	0.000	0.000

* Not elsewhere classified.

Table B.3. Likelihood of economies to import counterfeit products infringing Swiss IPR

GTRIC-e for destination economies, 2014-16

	2014	2015	2016
Afghanistan	0.00	0.00	0.00
Albania	0.00	0.00	0.00
Algeria	0.00	0.00	0.00
American Samoa	0.00	0.00	0.00
Andorra	0.00	0.00	0.00
Angola	0.05	0.05	0.06
Anguilla	0.00	0.00	0.00
Antarctica		0.00	
Antigua and Barbuda	0.00	0.00	0.00
Argentina	0.41	0.41	0.47
Armenia	0.00	0.00	0.00
Aruba	0.00	0.00	0.00
Australia	0.03	0.03	0.04
Austria	0.31	0.31	0.37
Azerbaijan	0.00	0.00	0.00
Bahamas	0.00	0.00	0.00
Bahrain	0.00	0.00	0.00
Bangladesh	0.00	0.00	0.00
Barbados	0.00	0.00	0.00
Belarus	0.00	0.00	0.00
Belgium	0.75	0.75	0.80
Belize	0.00	0.00	0.00
Benin	0.00	0.00	0.00
Bermuda	0.00	0.00	0.00
Bhutan	0.00	0.00	0.00
Bolivia	0.00	0.00	0.00
Bonaire	0.00	0.00	0.00
Bosnia and Herzegovina	0.00	0.00	0.00
Botswana	0.00	0.00	0.00
Bouvet Island	0.00	0.00	
Brazil	0.20	0.20	0.25
British Indian Ocean Territory	0.00		0.00
British Virgin Islands	0.00	0.00	0.00
Brunei Darussalam	0.00	0.00	0.00
Bulgaria	0.54	0.54	0.60
Burkina Faso	0.00	0.00	0.00
Burundi	0.00	0.00	0.00
Cabo Verde	0.00	0.00	0.00
Cambodia	0.00	0.00	0.00
Cameroon	0.43	0.43	0.50
Canada	0.06	0.06	0.08
Cayman Islands	0.00	0.00	0.00
Central African Republic	0.00	0.00	0.00
Chad	0.00	0.00	0.00

Chile	0.03	0.03	0.05
China (People's Republic of)	0.03	0.03	0.04
Christmas Island	0.00		0.00
Cocos (Keeling) Islands	0.00		
Colombia	0.03	0.03	0.05
Comoros	0.00	0.00	0.00
Congo	0.00	0.00	0.00
Cook Islands	0.00	0.00	0.00
Costa Rica	0.00	0.00	0.00
Côte d'Ivoire	0.00	0.00	0.00
Croatia	0.33	0.33	0.39
Cuba	0.00	0.00	0.00
Curaçao	0.00	0.00	0.00
Cyprus*	0.47	0.46	0.53
Czech Republic	0.44	0.44	0.51
Democratic People's Republic of Korea	0.00	0.00	0.00
Democratic Republic of the Congo	0.13	0.13	0.16
Denmark	0.93	0.93	0.95
Djibouti	0.00	0.00	0.00
Dominica	0.00	0.00	0.00
Dominican Republic	0.03	0.03	0.04
Ecuador	0.00	0.00	0.00
Egypt	0.00	0.00	0.00
El Salvador	0.00	0.00	0.00
Equatorial Guinea	0.00	0.00	0.00
Eritrea	0.00	0.00	0.00
Estonia	0.47	0.47	0.53
Ethiopia	0.00	0.00	0.00
Falkland Islands (Malvinas)	0.00	0.00	0.00
Faroe Islands	0.00	0.00	0.00
Fiji	0.00	0.00	0.00
Finland	0.11	0.11	0.14
Former Yugoslav Republic of Macedonia	0.00	0.00	0.00
France	0.42	0.42	0.48
French Polynesia	0.00	0.00	0.00
French Southern and Antarctic Lands	0.00	0.00	0.00
Gabon	0.31	0.31	0.37
Gambia	0.00	0.00	0.00
Georgia	0.00	0.00	0.00
Germany	0.44	0.44	0.50
Ghana	0.00	0.00	0.00
Gibraltar	0.00	0.00	0.00
Greece	0.46	0.45	0.52
Greenland	0.00	0.00	0.00
Grenada	0.00	0.00	0.00
Guam	0.00	0.00	0.00
Guatemala	0.00	0.00	0.00
Guinea	0.02	0.02	0.03
Guinea-Bissau	0.00	0.00	0.00
Guyana	0.00	0.00	0.00
Haiti	0.00	0.00	0.00
Holy See	0.00	0.00	0.00
Honduras	0.08	0.08	0.10
Hong Kong (China)	0.00	0.00	0.00
Hungary	0.42	0.42	0.48
Iceland	0.03	0.03	0.04
India	0.03	0.03	0.04

Indonesia	0.00	0.00	0.00
Iran	0.00	0.00	0.00
Iraq	0.00	0.00	0.00
Ireland	0.43	0.43	0.49
Israel	0.03	0.03	0.04
Italy	0.32	0.32	0.38
Jamaica	0.00	0.00	0.00
Japan	0.10	0.10	0.13
Jordan	0.00	0.00	0.00
Kazakhstan	0.00	0.00	0.00
Kenya	0.03	0.03	0.04
Kiribati	0.00	0.00	0.00
Korea	0.07	0.07	0.10
Kuwait	0.11	0.11	0.14
Kyrgyzstan	0.00	0.00	0.00
Lao People's Democratic Republic	0.00	0.00	0.00
Latvia	0.65	0.65	0.71
Lebanon	0.00	0.00	0.00
Lesotho	0.00	0.00	0.00
Liberia	0.00	0.00	0.00
Libya	0.00	0.00	0.00
Lithuania	0.26	0.26	0.31
Luxembourg	0.92	0.92	0.94
Macau (China)	0.00	0.00	0.00
Madagascar	0.00	0.00	0.00
Malawi	0.00	0.00	0.00
Malaysia	0.00	0.00	0.00
Maldives	0.00	0.00	0.00
Mali	0.04	0.04	0.05
Malta	0.93	0.93	0.95
Marshall Islands	0.00	0.00	0.00
Mauritania	0.00	0.00	0.00
Mauritius	0.00	0.00	0.00
Mexico	0.03	0.03	0.04
Micronesia	0.00	0.00	0.00
Moldova	0.00	0.00	0.00
Mongolia	0.00	0.00	0.00
Montenegro	0.00	0.00	0.00
Montserrat	0.00	0.00	0.00
Morocco	0.46	0.46	0.52
Mozambique	0.00	0.00	0.00
Myanmar	0.00	0.00	0.00
Namibia	0.00	0.00	0.00
Nauru	0.00	0.00	
Nepal	0.00	0.00	0.00
Netherlands	0.32	0.32	0.38
New Caledonia	0.00	0.00	0.00
New Zealand	0.00	0.00	0.00
Nicaragua	0.00	0.00	0.00
Niger	0.00	0.00	0.00
Nigeria	0.14	0.14	0.18
Niue		0.00	0.00
Norfolk Island	0.00	0.00	
Northern Mariana Islands	0.00	0.00	0.00
Norway	0.13	0.13	0.17
Oman	0.00	0.00	0.00
Pakistan	0.00	0.00	0.00

Palau	0.00	0.00	0.00
Palestinian Authority*	0.00	0.00	0.00
Panama	0.00	0.00	0.00
Papua New Guinea	0.00	0.00	0.00
Paraguay	0.06	0.06	0.09
Peru	0.03	0.03	0.05
Philippines	0.00	0.00	0.00
Poland	0.35	0.35	0.41
Portugal	0.89	0.89	0.92
Qatar	0.05	0.05	0.07
Romania	0.32	0.31	0.37
Russia	0.06	0.06	0.08
Rwanda	0.00	0.00	0.00
Saint-Barthélemy	0.00	0.00	0.00
Saint Helena	0.00	0.00	
Saint Kitts and Nevis	0.00	0.00	0.00
Saint Lucia	0.00	0.00	0.00
Saint Vincent and the Grenadines	0.00	0.00	0.00
Samoa	0.00	0.00	0.00
San Marino	0.00	0.00	0.00
Sao Tome and Principe	0.00	0.00	0.00
Saudi Arabia	0.03	0.03	0.04
Senegal	0.00	0.00	0.00
Serbia	0.20	0.20	0.24
Seychelles	0.00	0.00	0.00
Sierra Leone	0.00	0.00	0.00
Singapore	0.00	0.00	0.00
Saint Maarten	0.00	0.00	0.00
Slovak Republic	0.25	0.25	0.30
Slovenia	0.71	0.71	0.76
Solomon Islands	0.00	0.00	0.00
Somalia	0.00	0.00	0.00
South Africa	0.00	0.00	0.00
South Georgia and the South Sandwich Islands	0.00	0.00	0.00
South Sudan	0.00	0.00	0.00
Spain	0.83	0.83	0.86
Sri Lanka	0.00	0.00	0.00
Sudan	0.00	0.00	0.00
Suriname	0.00	0.00	0.00
Swaziland	0.00	0.00	0.00
Sweden	0.52	0.52	0.58
Syrian Arab Republic	0.00	0.00	0.00
Tajikistan	0.00	0.00	0.00
Tanzania	0.29	0.29	0.35
Thailand	0.03	0.03	0.04
Timor-Leste	0.00	0.00	0.00
Togo	0.00	0.00	0.00
Tonga	0.00	0.00	0.00
Trinidad and Tobago	0.00	0.00	0.00
Tunisia	0.00	0.00	0.00
Turkey	0.03	0.03	0.04
Turkmenistan	0.00	0.00	0.00
Turks and Caicos Islands	0.00	0.00	0.00
Tuvalu	0.00	0.00	0.00
Uganda	0.00	0.00	0.00
Ukraine	0.06	0.06	0.09
United Arab Emirates	0.10	0.10	0.13

United Kingdom	0.60	0.60	0.66
United States	0.21	0.21	0.26
United States Minor Outlying Islands	0.00	0.00	0.00
Uruguay	0.20	0.20	0.25
Uzbekistan	0.00	0.00	0.00
Vanuatu	0.00	0.00	0.00
Venezuela	0.07	0.07	0.09
Viet Nam	0.00	0.00	0.00
Yemen	0.11	0.11	0.14
Zambia	0.00	0.00	0.00
Zimbabwe	0.00	0.00	0.00

Note: * The information in this document with reference to "Cyprus" relates to the southern part of the Island. There is no single authority representing both Turkish and Greek Cypriot people on the Island. Turkey recognises the Turkish Republic of Northern Cyprus (TRNC). Until a lasting and equitable solution is found within the context of the UN, Turkey shall preserve its position concerning the "Cyprus issue".
The Republic of Cyprus is recognised by all members of the UN with the exception of Turkey. The information in this document relates to the area under the effective control of the Government of the Republic of Cyprus.

Table B.4. Industries by Harmonised System (HS) codes

HS code	Description
01	Live animals.
02	Meat and edible meat offal.
03	Fish and crustaceans, molluscs and other aquatic invertebrates.
04	Dairy produce; birds' eggs; natural honey; edible products of animal origin, not elsewhere specified or included.
05	Products of animal origin, not elsewhere specified or included.
06	Live trees and other plants; bulbs, roots and the like; cut flowers and ornamental foliage.
07	Edible vegetables and certain roots and tubers.
08	Edible fruit and nuts; peel of citrus fruit or melons.
09	Coffee, tea, mate and spices.
10	Cereals.
11	Products of the milling industry; malt; starches; inulin; wheat gluten.
12	Oil seeds and oleaginous fruits; miscellaneous grains, seeds and fruit; industrial or medicinal plants; straw and fodder.
13	Lac; gums, resins and other vegetable saps and extracts.
14	Vegetable plaiting materials; vegetable products not elsewhere specified or included.
15	Animal or vegetable fats and oils and their cleavage products; prepared edible fats; animal or vegetable waxes.
16	Preparations of meat, fish or crustaceans, molluscs or other aquatic invertebrates.
17	Sugars and sugar confectionery.
18	Cocoa and cocoa preparations.
19	Preparations of cereals, flour, starch or milk; pastry cooks' products.
20	Preparations of vegetables, fruit, nuts or other parts of plants.
21	Miscellaneous edible preparations.
22	Beverages, spirits and vinegar.
23	Residues and waste from the food industries; prepared animal fodder.
24	Tobacco and manufactured tobacco substitutes.
25	Salt; sulphur; earth and stone; plastering materials, lime and cement.
26	Ores, slag and ash.
27	Mineral fuels, mineral oils and products of their distillation; bituminous substances; mineral waxes.
28	Inorganic chemicals; organic or inorganic compounds of precious metals, rare-earth metals, radioactive elements or isotopes.

HS code	Description
29	Organic chemicals.
30	Pharmaceutical products.
31	Fertilisers.
32	Tanning or dyeing extracts; tannins and their derivatives; dyes, pigments and other colouring matter; paints and varnishes; putty and other mastics; inks.
33	Essential oils and resinoids; perfumery, cosmetic or toilet preparations.
34	Soap, organic surface-active agents, washing preparations, lubricating preparations, artificial waxes, prepared waxes, polishing or scouring preparations, candles and similar articles, modelling pastes, "dental waxes" and dental preparations
35	Albuminoidal substances; modified starches; glues; enzymes.
36	Explosives; pyrotechnic products; matches; pyrophoric alloys; certain combustible preparations.
37	Photographic or cinematographic goods.
38	Miscellaneous chemical products.
39	Plastics and articles thereof.
40	Rubber and articles thereof.
41	Raw hides and skins (other than fur skins) and leather.
42	Articles of leather; saddlery and harness; travel goods, handbags and similar containers; articles of animal gut (other than silkworm gut).
43	Fur skins and artificial fur; manufactures thereof.
44	Wood and articles of wood; wood charcoal.
45	Cork and articles of cork.
46	Manufactures of straw, of esparto or other plaiting materials; basketware and wickerwork.
47	Pulp of wood or other fibrous cellulosic material; recovered (waste and scrap) paper or paperboard.
48	Paper and paperboard; articles of paper pulp, of paper or paperboard.
49	Printed books, newspapers, pictures and other products of the printing industry; manuscripts, typescripts and plans.
50	Silk.
51	Wool, fine or coarse animal hair; horsehair yarn and woven fabric.
52	Cotton.
53	Other vegetable textile fibres; paper yarn and woven fabrics of paper yarn.
54	Man-made filaments.
55	Man-made staple fibres.
56	Wadding, felt and nonwovens; special yarns; twine, cordage, ropes and cables and articles thereof.
57	Carpets and other textile floor coverings.
58	Special woven fabrics; tufted textile fabrics; lace; tapestries; trimmings; embroidery.
59	Impregnated, coated, covered or laminated textile fabrics; textile articles of a kind suitable for industrial use.
60	Knitted or crocheted fabrics.
61	Articles of apparel and clothing accessories, knitted or crocheted.
62	Articles of apparel and clothing accessories, not knitted or crocheted.
63	Other made up textile articles; sets; worn clothing and worn textile articles; rags.
64	Footwear, gaiters and the like; parts of such articles.
65	Headgear and parts thereof.
66	Umbrellas, sun umbrellas, walking-sticks, seat-sticks, whips, riding-crops and parts thereof.
67	Prepared feathers and down and articles made of feathers or down; artificial flowers; articles of human hair.
68	Articles of stone, plaster, cement, asbestos, mica or similar materials.
69	Ceramic products.
70	Glass and glassware.

HS code	Description
71	Natural or cultured pearls, precious or semi-precious stones, precious metals, metals clad with precious metal and articles thereof; imitation, jewellery; coin.
72	Iron and steel.
73	Articles of iron or steel.
74	Copper and articles thereof.
75	Nickel and articles thereof.
76	Aluminium and articles thereof.
77	(Reserved for possible future use in the Harmonised System)
78	Lead and articles thereof.
79	Zinc and articles thereof.
80	Tin and articles thereof.
81	Other base metals; cermets; articles thereof.
82	Tools, implements, cutlery, spoons and forks, of base metal; parts thereof of base metal.
83	Miscellaneous articles of base metal.
84	Nuclear reactors, boilers, machinery and mechanical appliances; parts thereof.
85	Electrical machinery and equipment and parts thereof; sound recorders and reproducers, television image and sound recorders and reproducers, and parts and accessories of such articles.
86	Railway or tramway locomotives, rolling stock and parts thereat railway or tramway track fixtures and fittings and parts thereof; mechanical (including electro-mechanical) traffic signalling equipment of all kinds.
87	Vehicles other than railway or tramway rolling stock, and parts and accessories thereof.
88	Aircraft, spacecraft and parts thereof.
89	Ships, boats and floating structures.
90	Optical, photographic, cinematographic, measuring, checking, precision, medical or surgical instruments and apparatus; parts and accessories thereof.
91	Clocks and watches and parts thereof.
92	Musical instruments; parts and accessories of such articles.
93	Arms and ammunition; parts and accessories thereof.
94	Furniture; bedding, mattresses, mattress supports, cushions and similar stuffed furnishings; lamps and lighting fittings, not elsewhere specified or included; illuminated signs, illuminated nameplates and the like; prefabricated buildings.
95	Toys, games and sports requisites; parts and accessories thereof.
96	Miscellaneous manufactured articles.
97	Works of art, collectors' pieces and antiques.
98	(Reserved for special uses by contracting parties).